ENDORSEMENTS

"I first met John Perry in the spring of 2000. I was looking for an offensive line/strength coach. We worked together for one year at Wayne County High School. I left and went to Northeast Community College and took John with me. In forty years of coaching, he's one of the best assistants I had. Not only from a coaching aspect, but what he did for kids outside of football. In conclusion, John Perry is one of the best humans I've known in seventy years on this earth."

— **BOBBY HALL,** *Hall of Fame Football Coach*

■ ■ ■

"Coach Perry doesn't just build football teams, he builds men of character, resilience, and emotional strength. This book is a powerful look inside the mindset and leadership that have shaped one of the most intentional cultures I've ever worked with."

— **ANGIE WILEY,** *Mental Performance Coach*

■ ■ ■

"Coach Perry is driven by the desire to get better—not just some of the time, but all the time. He is passionate about the process of helping everyone become the best they can be. Whether it is working on his podcast or teaching his leadership class, he has laser beam focus on getting better and making those around him better. If you really want to get better every day, read this book."

— **RICK JONES,** *Assistant to the Head Coach,*
University of Missouri Football

"John Perry is my go-to source for guidance in personal development and mental performance training. His ability to translate complex concepts into practical actions has shaped the way I coach, lead, and live."
— **CHRIS YEAGER,** *Head Football Coach, Mountain Brook High School*

■ ■ ■

"Blending powerful storytelling with a humble, no-nonsense approach, Coach John Perry has a rare ability to spark something in others that compels them to show up better for themselves, their families, their workplaces, and their communities."
— **LOGAN AGUIRRE,** *owner and publisher,* 417 Magazine

■ ■ ■

"A RIDDLE: What do you get when one of the best football coaches in America who is also a world-class storyteller puts all he has into a book??? You get an incredibly entertaining, interesting, and exciting book that you won't be able to put down!!!
A GUARANTEE: You will LOVE this book!"
— **ROB GILBERT,** *PhD, professor of sports psychology at Montclair State University and host of the* Success Hotline

■ ■ ■

"Coach Perry has mastered the art of storytelling to bring energy, leadership insight, and a wealth of knowledge as a well-studied football coach who has a deep love of personal growth. He is unexpected, an enigma, a tough coach who cares about the development of his team off the field so they can perform at their highest level on the field—and in life."
— **JOSELYN BALDNER,** *chief executive officer of Central Bank*

"I've had the privilege of knowing Coach Perry as both a friend and a leader, and what separates him is simple—he lives what he teaches. John is a daily reader, a lifelong learner, and someone who believes that when you grow yourself, you elevate everyone around you.

John doesn't just talk about being a Coffee Bean—he embodies it. I've watched him bring the Coffee Bean message into multiple cities, changing environments by the way he shows up and leads. This book reflects who he is: intentional growth, daily discipline, and a heart for helping others become better than they were yesterday."

— DAMON WEST, *best-selling coauthor of* The Coffee Bean

■ ■ ■

"I've known John for more than twenty-five years, and I've watched him consistently build programs the right way—through culture, relationships, and daily standards. This book is John at his best: honest, intentional, and rooted in the belief that when you build a great culture, everything else has a chance to flourish."

— WILL HALL, *Head Football Coach, Tulane University*

■ ■ ■

"I've known John for many years, and what he's built at Nixa is a direct reflection of who he is—intentional, disciplined, and relentlessly committed to growth. This book captures the same mindset he instills in his program: develop the person, elevate the standard, and the results will follow."

— DAN LANNING, *Head Football Coach, University of Oregon*

■ ■ ■

"Coach Perry has built Nixa Football into a program defined by growth, discipline, and belief, and that shows up in the way his players are prepared to compete at the next level. He doesn't just coach football—he develops young men and relentlessly advocates for his athletes, and college coaches across the region have taken notice."
— ELI DRINKWITZ, *Head Football Coach, University of Missouri*

NEVER STOP GETTING BETTER

NEVER STOP GETTING BETTER

BECOMING WHO YOU WERE MEANT TO BE

JOHN PERRY

NEVER STOP GETTING BETTER
Becoming Who You Were Meant to Be

Cover Design by Abigael Elliott
Interior Layout and Design by Brittany Becker
Editorial Team: Hallie Knox, Rachel Maier, Jeff Glauser, Tessa Carvalho

ISBNs:
E-book: 979-8-89165-396-2
Paperback: 979-8-89165-395-5
Hardcover: 979-8-89165-394-8

Published by:
Streamline
Kansas City, MO
shareyourstory.com

*I dedicate this book to my parents,
whose love, support, and example shaped
the foundation of who I am today.*

*And to my family—
Stephanie, my soulmate, thank you for your constant
encouragement and belief in me.
Haley and J, thank you for your love and grace
that mean more than you know.*

CONTENTS

PART 1: BUILD THE FOUNDATION

PART 2: BUILD THE HABITS

FOREWORD

DO YOU WANT to grow to your next level—for REAL? Reading this book—underlining, highlighting, tabbing pages, and acting on what you learn—will get you on the path to your next level, and possibly beyond.

But that depends on you. Are you coachable and ready to train yourself to Never Stop Getting Better (NSGB)?

I first heard Coach John Perry speak in February 2020 at the Nixa High School Library after he had just been announced as the new head varsity football coach for the Eagles. His southern Mississippi talk was familiar, as my wife was born in Mississippi, and her side of our family lives in LA (lower Alabama).

Coach Perry cast the vision of building the best football program and young leaders in the state of Missouri. He spoke with a combination of humility and confidence, two powerful traits of a great leader. He also spoke with clarity and certainty as he shared some of his past and what we could create together at Nixa. Little did he know the level of uncertainty about to hit our great country that year in mid-March 2020—the beginning of the COVID-19 lockdown. No challenge in the vision he just cast, even with a country full of uncertainty, tension, and turmoil. He was here to get better, and to bring others with him on that journey—no matter the obstacles.

Our middle son, Reid, was the senior starting quarterback during Coach Perry's first year. Another obstacle for Coach that first regular season: Reid tore his ACL during a summer practice. Reid rehabbed and did end up playing the last five games with that torn ACL, and Coach Perry's first season with the Nixa Eagles went into the playoffs. He coached them to a three-point loss to the eventual state championship team, playing them closer than anyone in the playoffs that year. The Nixa Eagles got better in their first year thanks to Coach Perry's leadership. He kept great coaches and brought on more great coaches to lead this program to the next level.

John and I connected early after his arrival; we had common interests in growth-focused books, podcasts, and trainings. After his first season with the Eagles, he asked if I would consider being a non-teaching assistant football coach with the varsity Eagles. I wanted to say yes instantly, but I needed to confirm with my work and my wife that I could cover the responsibilities for all of it. My high school coaches changed my life; heck, Coach Bob Price saved my life! I am a big fan of coaches and the positive and lifelong impact they can have on young people. I said yes.

Other than Miss Stephanie, or "Sugar," as Georgia calls her, over the last five years I have probably gotten to know John Perry as well as or better than anyone. We have become friends, coached together, gotten certified in Mental Performance Mastery together, and grown businesses alongside each other, businesses that are focused on one thing—helping people grow.

It's one thing to learn professional growth skills in order to lead a team. It's another level when someone intentionally and consistently combines that professional growth with personal growth. I have seen John challenge himself in many ways, and I have also seen life challenge John in many ways. My wife and I have grown close to John and his wife Stephanie, daughter Haley, son J, and granddaughter Georgia. We have seen their family not only go through challenges but grow through those challenges too. John has worked on growing as a husband and a dad. Stephanie has grown (although she said she wasn't going to, lol). We have seen Haley grow through challenges, becoming a great mom, and witnessed J work hard to be good enough to get into one of the top universities in the country for theater (a different path than Dad). We are all different. And we can all grow, especially if we are blessed to have parents, coaches, mentors, or others grow in front of us as an example of hope and possibility.

We are all always a work in progress—me, John, you, everyone. Professionally, John continues to grow as a football coach, a speaker, a podcaster, and now a writer. He is living the higher level of growth by giving from that growth. He is serving others—one of his three core values.

What if you could Never Stop Getting Better at________________ (you fill in the blank).

What if you could become a better person, spouse, parent, coach, leader, mentor, and friend? You can if you read and apply Coach Perry's lessons, stories, and truths in this book.

To grow, you must become aware and accept that discomfort is part of the process.

Growing is hard. Not growing is harder! Choose your pain wisely. I would recommend stepping into the training in this book with the mindset of, "I *get* to, *choose* to, *love* to do hard things."

As it says in James 1:2–4, *"Consider it pure joy, my brothers and sisters, whenever you face trials of many kinds, because you know that the testing of your faith produces perseverance. Let perseverance finish its work so that you may be mature and complete, not lacking anything."*

The next verse makes this promise even more powerful if you are willing to seek, ask, and find . . .

You are wonderfully made and one of a kind. There is one thing in life that absolutely no one in the world can do better than you: become a better you. Only you can do that. There has never been another you before you. There is not another you on the planet today. And there will never be another you.

When you get better—the world gets better.

When you get better—you are more equipped to serve the person you once were.

When you get better—it is a powerful example to those who experience your growth.

When you choose to Never Stop Getting Better—you become a great steward of the life God has given you.

Read, journal, and reflect on where you are now. Embrace discomfort and become aware of what is possible. Continuously learn how to get better to grow, and then forever intentionally transfer what you learn and live to serve and challenge others to do the same. When your growth eventually impacts the growth of another person, that is the REAL FIT Life! Then, like Coach Perry, you will Never Stop Getting Better.

You are worth it, and you absolutely have what it takes to Never Stop Getting Better.

God bless your attitude, your focus, your effort, and your response to all the opportunities coming your way from learning and applying what you read here.

—CHANCE POTTS

Friend, coach, entrepreneur, and fellow NSGB team member

INTRODUCTION

I F YOU'D TOLD me thirty years ago that one day I'd be writing a book about personal growth, mindset, and mental fitness, I'd have told you to quit lying. If you'd told as much to my old Harding University teammate Paul Simmons, he'd have said the same thing. In fact, Paul *did* say it.

On my podcast not too long ago, this is what he shared:

> There are very few people I've been teammates with whom I'm as proud of as John Perry. I say that because my initial perception of him was simple: a Mississippi Junior College product, offensive lineman, loud, a good ol' boy.
>
> And if somebody would have told me, "Hey, Coach, you need to know that in twenty years, John Perry is going to be a wildly successful, state championship-winning football coach," that really wouldn't have surprised me.
>
> But if you would have said, "He also is an amazing leader of men. He is crazy well read, he is really intentional,

he walks daily, he impacts other coaches; his leadership is elite."

If I would have heard those things, I would have said, "No, that's a different John Perry."[1]

Today, I take those words as a compliment, and ten times over because it's coming from Paul, who is now leading one of the best Division II programs in the United States, Harding University. He's right about one thing, for sure: I *am* a different John Perry. Thank you, Jesus!

That's the whole point of this book. I can change. You can change. Anybody can change. You can get better—*a lot* better—if you decide to. We have two choices daily: get better or get worse. That choice is yours and mine to make.

I've spent over thirty years coaching high school football, and in that time, I've learned that the game is really just a big old metaphor for life. You either grow or you stay stuck. You either get sharper or you get dull. You either learn to keep showing up, or life benches you.

I had the privilege of leading my alma mater, Pearl High School, to its first-ever state championship in 2017. We went 16–0 that year—only the third team in Mississippi history to do so. In 2018, I became the winningest coach in Pearl's history, leading the team to 101 victories. It was a dream come true.

And then, my wife and I felt like God was leading us in a different direction, toward a new challenge. After spending twelve years coaching at my alma mater—and can I just say, those were twelve of the best years of my life—we decided to move our family to Nixa, Missouri, where we didn't know a soul, to start life from scratch once again.

Now, after six seasons as head coach at Nixa, we've gone 64–11, won four conference titles and three district championships, and finished as the Class 6 state runner-up twice. I've coached in the Under Armour All-America Game, started a podcast, trained as a certified mental performance coach, and spoken to businesses all over Missouri. I'm saying all this not to boast or say, "Look how special I am!" but to make this point: If a boy from Pearl, Mississippi, who scored an 18 on the ACT can change and succeed like that, then *so can you*. Anyone can get better. No one is trapped. We all have the choice.

And that's what this book's about. To challenge you, as I challenge myself each day, to Never Stop Getting Better (NSGB)—to become the best version of yourself so you can show up for others in the best way possible. I'm writing this book in order to live out my core values of curiosity, making a difference, and serving others. And I'll show you how you can NSGB and live out your core values too. (More to come on those core values later.)

Each chapter is going to be short, digestible, and to the point—built around a story, a lesson, and a practice, activity, or mindset shift you can engage with *today*. I'll tell you the lessons I've learned through my own process of continuing to Never Stop Getting Better: What I've gleaned from the football field, from failure, from moving states, from mentors, from coaching thousands of young men, and from trying (and often failing) to live out what I teach. One of life's certainties is *life is hard*! We have all been through adversity, and it is a guaranteed fact that we will all go through *more* adversity in the future. We *must* get better, so that we can have the opportunity to thrive instead of merely survive when that next challenge hits.

In the pages to come, we'll talk about things like:

- how to break your habitual mindset cycle and take control of your thoughts (that's called neuroplasticity—don't worry, I'll make it make sense),
- how to control your responses and reject blaming, complaining, and defensiveness (BCD),
- how to set your eyes on what matters, creating a bold vision,
- how to build mental toughness and emotional control,
- how to conquer the edge,
- and loads more.

If you want to chase a better version of yourself, this book will give you the tools and the push to get there. We can do it together!

You can be *different*—whenever you decide you want to be. We all can become better versions of ourselves every day, if we choose to. The name of the game, in football and in life, is simple: Never Stop Getting Better.

PART 1

BUILD THE FOUNDATION

CHAPTER 1

THE MINDSET CYCLE

IN THE FALL of 2004, I was in my second season as the head football coach of a team (Kosciusko) that won only *two* games the year before I came on board. In year one, we won *nine* games, made the second round of the state playoffs, and I was named The Star-Herald's Newsmaker of the Year . . . So year two as a head coach was off to a great start! We were 5–1 and feeling great about ourselves, ranked in the top ten in the state.

In week seven, we headed to Canton, Mississippi, to take on a 3–3 team that had won only three games total the previous year. I would have described Canton as historically . . . unchallenging—but somehow, unexpectedly, we *lost*. 47–43. Mistakes were made all around. They could not stop us on offense, and we ran counter trap successfully all night, and likewise, *we* could not stop *them* on offense. We found ourselves in a shoot-out that night! Little did I know then that they had a great quarterback, Desmond Ratcliff, who would go on to be a junior college all-star and play four years of college ball. That night, he could have doubled as Michael Vick. He was very good, but we made him great.

To put it plainly, I feel we fumbled that game away. And afterward, I had plenty of blame to throw around. I pushed it all on the team. Nowadays, I've learned to take the blame myself when it goes badly; to give credit to the team when it goes well; and to give the other team credit for making the plays that won the game. But I was a different man then, and I had no set system for behavior and leadership!

I just wasn't the same person that I am today. I was, dare I say, an undisciplined human who could be a hothead, and all hell broke loose. The team had messed up. They had only themselves to blame for the loss, and I wanted my boys to understand that fact and to understand it *well*. In the end, I very nearly tanked my marriage over some post-game sandwiches.

My wife and a group of parents had made about two hundred sandwiches for the kids the night before. I headed straight to the buses with the intention of throwing them jokers in the dumpster, because I thought that *those boys didn't even deserve to eat*. My wife, Stephanie, was furious with me, of course, and adamant that the kids get their food. We had an all-out battle right there at the bus door, with her standing guard of the sandwiches and me cussing and throwing a pretty good fit! (In truth, the argument we put on was a better fight than our team had put up that night.)

To this day, I can't remember who technically "won" the argument, but I'm willing to bet those kids got to eat their sandwiches (probably while I sulked in a corner with my own big old serving of humble pie). Stephanie is nothing if not fierce and formidable, and I say that with a great deal of pride.

Now, my mindset has improved drastically since that day, though deep down, I think I'll always be a terrible loser. I definitely still hate to lose more than I love to win. But today when we lose a game, though it still hurts, I have a different mindset. Instead of throwing sandwiches and blaming the team, I work with the kids to apply the Army's AAR process: an After-Action Review. It's just five simple questions, but it takes the emotions out of the process, propels us to be better, and puts the emphasis on improving instead of complaining. That process can work wonders, as it shifts us out of sulking and into sharpening, out of complaint and into correction. We trade frustration for fascination and work to become curious in the place of furious. And, of course, *I* choose to take the blame! As the leader, it's on *me*!

That night in Canton, I wasn't good enough yet. But through mindset training, years of getting up early and reading, and putting myself around those that are further down the road, I've begun to learn this: It's not about the outcome—it's about the process. And above all else, I must keep getting better! #NSGB

We don't get the life we deserve. We get the life we focus on. Where our focus goes, our life grows!

And the good news is, we can all change what we focus on. That's neuroplasticity for you!

Wait, what's neuroplasticity again? I'll tell ya.

THE LESSON: BRAIN SCIENCE 101

Neuroplasticity is the brain's remarkable ability to reorganize itself by forming new neural connections, allowing it to adapt, learn, and be transformed throughout life.

The Bible already told us plainly, long ago: *"Do not conform to the pattern of this world, but be transformed by the renewing of your mind"* (Romans 12:2a).

Modern neuroscience is now catching up to Scripture, confirming that the life you live flows out of the thoughts you choose to manage—or fail to manage.

So, when I talk about breaking your mindset cycle, what *exactly* do I mean? Let's break it down in a little more detail:

- Your thoughts become your self-talk.
- Your self-talk shapes your emotions.

- Your emotions create your physiological state (heart rate, breathing, hormones).
- Your physiological state drives your behavior and performance.

None of us can control our every thought, but we *do* control our self-talk—that's the crucial "middle link" in the chain. That's the lever you can pull to redirect your mindset and your outcomes. In fact, of the four phases in the mindset cycle, we really *only* control our self-talk. The story we create and tell ourselves is the most important story ever. When a negative thought hits, all you have to do is ask two simple questions:

1. Is it true?
2. Is it helpful?

If it's not true, dismiss it and get a better one. If it *is* true, move to that second question. Ask yourself, "Is this thought serving me and adding value to me?" If not, reframe it into something that *does* serve, that *does* add value. Thoughts are just mental reps, so you've got to choose the reps that strengthen you.

How often must you do this? Over and over and over again. We can and should control the stories we tell ourselves. No other story in the world is more important than the story *we tell ourselves*. We do not control our thoughts; we are not our thoughts—but we *do* control what we do with our thoughts after we receive them. This is a skill we can get better at! Trust me on this one.

Here's some science that should wake us up:

- We have sixty thousand thoughts per day, and 90 percent of those thoughts are repetitive.[2]
- 80 percent of our thoughts are negative.[3]
- 47 percent of the time, your mind is wandering.[4]
- The average person spends 706 hours a year on social media (that's four and a half work months) and watches 2,700 hours of

TV, and the average twenty-one-year-old male has played 10,000 hours of video games.[5]

- The average smartphone user touches their phone 2,617 times a day (top 10 percent: more than 5,400 times).[6]
- Approximately 21 percent of US adults are experiencing some type of mental illness (anxiety, depression, trauma, bipolar disorder, etc.).[7]
- The average child today exhibits the same level of anxiety as the average psychiatric patient in the 1950s.[8]
- A 2017 study found that forty million adults eighteen years of age and older are battling an anxiety disorder.[9]

No wonder so many people feel mentally scattered. We've trained our brains to be reactive instead of resilient. And it's only going to get worse, with all the technology that continues to explode and take over our lives in this crazy world.

Luckily for us all, my unexpected life is a testimony to the fact that mindset *is* trainable. Neuroplasticity, again, means that you can literally rewire your brain! Each time you catch, question, and correct a thought, you're building stronger and better pathways. Over time, those pathways become patterned ways of thinking: your mindset.

As I love to say, you cannot be grateful and hateful at the same time! You've heard the old saying, "Is the glass half empty or half full?" I say, "Who cares? Can we just be grateful we have a glass?" Ha. Perspective is everything!

A fixed mindset says, "I am my thoughts."

A growth mindset says, "I can choose and train my thoughts."

That choice determines how you show up in every moment of your life.

THE CHALLENGE: REWRITE THE CYCLE

1. ***Pick a mantra:*** Choose a phrase that resets your cycle when thoughts spiral. Examples:
   - So what? Now what?
   - Everything is working for my good.
   - What's important *right now*?
   - Never Stop Getting Better.
   - I will control my response.

2. ***Implement the AARs:*** After your next setback (big or small), apply the Army's five-question After-Action Review. Ask yourself:
   - What were the intended results?
   - What were the actual results?
   - What caused the results?
   - What will we do the same next time?
   - What will we do differently?

3. ***Track your self-talk:*** For one week, journal when you catch a negative thought and how you reframed it. Begin training your brain like you train your body.

CHAPTER 2

FAILURE DOESN'T EXIST

AFTER I GRADUATED from Harding University back in 1994, my high school coach Bruce Merchant (Hall of Fame 2012) called me up to offer me a job at Pearl High School—my alma mater—as the offensive line coach. What an opportunity: to return to my high school and start my coaching career on the Class 5 level! I jumped at the chance to go back and coach alongside all the guys who once coached *me*. Coach Bruce Merchant is still one of the most influential men in my life, and I'm very thankful to have played for *and* coached with him. Truly one of the greats! I will forever be indebted to him. The Merchants *are* Pearl football!

But Bruce resigned in the spring of 1998, and Pearl High School hired a hotshot young coach, Marcus Boyles. Marcus had a record of 67–4 and had already won two state championships at Taylorsville High School. He was absolutely phenomenal! I was beyond excited to get the opportunity to coach alongside and learn from him, as he was one of the absolute best to ever walk the sidelines in the state of Mississippi. We all had to interview in order to keep our jobs at the time, and he decided who to keep and who to let go. My interview went well; I kept my offensive line title and added strength and conditioning (as well as powerlifting) to my job description.

I was so pumped, and life was so good.

Then, in the spring of 2000, Marcus left, taking a new job as the offensive coordinator at Wayne County High School. This time, Pearl ended up hiring Larry Weems to replace him—another in a long line of very successful Pearl football coaches.

Truth be told, I wasn't thrilled when Larry was hired. Nothing personal at all—I just didn't know him. I was friends with our defensive coordinator, Joey Ezelle, and *he* had applied for the head coach position. All of us assistants were rooting for Joey, so when he wasn't hired, it felt like a slap in the face. Looking back, I am sure the administration just wanted a clean slate, but—fair or not—that's how we felt about it at the time.

Each of us had to interview again in order to keep our jobs, but this time, I was much less pumped. Entitlement had set in, and I thought I was hot stuff, that Larry would be lucky to have me, and that he would be begging me to stay. Little did I know, Larry hadn't heard the first thing about me and really didn't care how high my opinion of myself was.

I interviewed, and personally, I thought it went really well. I got called back for a second interview, but as I'd soon find out, I was being called in to be fired.

My friend and fellow coach, Kyle Hammond, was pulling out of the parking lot just as I pulled into the parking lot for the meeting. We passed each other on the road, and I found out later that he had just been fired as well. If I had arrived a few minutes earlier and met Kyle while he was walking out, I probably never would have gone in that day at all. I would have realized that if they were firing him, I was next.

Anyway, I walked into the high school principal's office, where all the meetings were being held, and my life changed forever. I showed up a cocky offensive line coach and walked out a humiliated human.

I am a Pearl boy. My family moved there when I was in the third grade, and I had no plans of ever leaving the town. But instead of getting the good news that I'd be keeping my job in my hometown, I made that two-mile trek home to tell my wife and our two-year-old little girl that I had just been fired and that we needed to figure out where we were headed next. Wow, what a switch of emotions in such a short amount of time. Talk about being in the valley, between mountains, or finding yourself in the ditch. I was there!

It was a very hard time for us as a family. Change is hard, and Pearl was all that I had really known. Other than the time I spent in college, I had never lived anywhere else.

As it turned out, Marcus Boyles knew that Bobby Hall (who had been his high school football coach) was looking for an offensive line coach at Wayne County (where Marcus had just taken that position as offensive coordinator). I went down for an interview, and Bobby and I hit it off! He was the most successful coach in the state of Mississippi (Hall of Fame 2017, with well over three hundred wins), and I wound up having the incredible opportunity to coach with him.

It was absolutely amazing. We took that program from just two wins the year before to ten in our first year! And I was coaching alongside some of the greats: Marcus Boyles and Bobby Hall, in the flesh. It was a better situation than I could have ever dreamed. I was in hog heaven, as O-line coaches like to say!

After one year at Wayne County, Bobby Hall had the opportunity to move back closer to his hometown and become the head football coach at Northeast Community College. He asked me to go with him, and I was absolutely thrilled to have the opportunity. We spent two wonderful years in Booneville, Mississippi, and then Coach Hall retired. Stephanie and I found ourselves back on the market looking for a job again, and we were extremely blessed to quickly land at Kosciusko High School for my first head coaching job. I will forever be grateful to the late Dr. David Sistrunk for trusting me and giving me the opportunity to be a head football coach!

Five years later, in 2008, Pearl called and offered me the opportunity to come home as the first Pearl graduate to be the head football coach in the history of the school. Mr. Pearl himself, Ray Rogers, would go on to always brag on the fact that Pearl High School had one of their own at the helm. He was so proud, and so was I. Life had come full circle. It all had worked out better than I ever could have planned it myself.

What I started to see from this long journey, with all its unexpected twists and turns, not fully understanding yet, was that God is always working. You must walk through the valley to see the mountains.

THE LESSON: SHIFT YOUR LENS

As Kobe Bryant once said, "Failure doesn't exist." He viewed setbacks as steps in the learning process, not as final outcomes. During the 2015 BET Experience Genius Talk (YouTube it!), Kobe sat down with Jemele Hill for a wide-ranging conversation about his career, mindset, and legacy. That conversation is fantastic, truly a master class for Never Stop Getting Better! When Hill asked him about the time he shot five air balls in a playoff game as a rookie, asking him what he thought about that failure, Kobe responded with, "What is failure?" He acted as if the word didn't even exist. He was actually tickled by the question. He explained that the only true failure would be to quit.

If you do not quit, you cannot fail. You can only learn and grow. *Win* or *learn*; the choice is yours.

What was absolutely one of the worst days of my entire life—that day when I got fired from Pearl—ultimately turned into one of the very best days in my life. If I hadn't been fired, I never would have gotten to work alongside two Hall of Fame coaches! God was blessing me, whether I liked how that blessing started or not. *We have to go through the valley to get to the mountain.*

As Romans 8:28 says, *"And we know that in all things God works for the good of those who love him, who have been called according to his purpose."*

What if we all had the ability to look at current negative situations and think, "This is an opportunity for something better to come into my life"? What if we asked, "God, what door are you opening for me now?"

How many of you can look back on a very negative event that happened in your life and now see the blessing that came out of it? I firmly believe that this is how God works. He allows us to go through the fire so we can be molded into what he wants us to be. Proverbs 17:3 puts it like this: *"The crucible for silver and the furnace for gold, but the Lord tests the heart."*

I love this Scripture because it reminds me of how gold is made. It is put into the furnace in its original state. The temperature is turned up and the impurities rise; they are removed, and the temperature is turned up some more. As more impurities rise, they are also removed, and the heat continues to be turned up, again and again, until all the impurities are gone. This is how God works in our lives. We have to go into the furnace to become the best version of ourselves, which is what he wants and is his plan.

There are blessings in disguise all around us, if only we can learn to shift our lens. Once we're able to reframe the adversities we face, we'll become able to truly learn, and to truly move forward to becoming the best version of ourselves.

THE CHALLENGE: FLIP THE SCRIPT

Time to engage with a written reflection that'll help you "flip the script."

1. Sit down with something to write with: pencil and paper, your phone, your computer.
2. Think about a noteworthy bad moment from your past. Write about what happened.
3. Trace that moment up through where you are now. Consider these questions:

a. What unexpected blessings arose from it?

b. How did it contribute to you becoming who you are today?

c. What do you have today that you never would have otherwise gained or experienced?

d. What was the ultimate lesson God wanted to teach you?

CHAPTER 3

E + R = O

I N 2016, I went to a coaching clinic where Brian Kight was speaking. I'd read and liked some stuff by his dad, Tim Kight, an author and well-respected leadership expert—and there was his son sitting on stage alongside the general manager of the Green Bay Packers! I figured the clinic was going to be good. Turns out it would be *more* than good: It was going to be one of the most impactful things I'd ever been a part of, and it would change my entire life.

Brian took leadership questions from the audience for over an hour, and his answers were spot on—just amazing. He is a leadership and performance coach who teaches something called the R Factor (his dad, Tim, coached the R Factor for over forty years as well before his recent passing). In part, the idea both Kight men really focus on is built around a simple equation: Event + Response = Outcome, or E + R = O.

I was floored by Brian's answers to the questions people asked him on stage that day. Absolutely blown away. He had two more breakout sessions over the next couple of days, and I eagerly attended both. I remember listening and just thinking, "*This is it.* This is the missing piece I've been looking for as a coach, as a leader, and honestly as a husband and father too!"

I started listening to the Kights' podcast every single day. It was called Focus 3, and there were about eighty episodes at the time. I truly think that I listened to one podcast episode a day over the next eighty days straight. I loved it! I couldn't get enough. I jumped into some of Brian's virtual courses and any other content I could find too. I even ended up contacting him and bringing him to Mississippi for our annual coaches' clinic to share him with all our coaches, developing a relationship with him that exists to this day.

The gist of the E + R = O learning that I gleaned during all that listening is this: You don't control the events that happen to you, and you don't directly control the outcomes of those events either. What you *do* control is your response. The better your response, the more influence you can have over the outcome. That's it. Life-changing.

The R Factor gives you six steps to strengthen your "response muscle." I am a systems guy. Give me some steps and I can figure it out. So when something happens, and you're trying to temper that immediate negative reaction, to interrupt it and change it into something else, here's what you do:

1. *Pause.* (Interrupt the emotion. Create space to think.)
2. *Get your mind right.* (Choose your mindset intentionally.)
3. *Step up.* (Make the disciplined choice, not the default one.)
4. *Adjust and adapt.* (Life changes; so must your approach.)
5. *Make a difference.* (Respond in ways that elevate others.)
6. *Build skill.* (Learn. Improve. Get better every day.)

Taking that idea and process to heart has changed how I coach and parent. It changed how I react to delays in traffic and at airports, to dealing with my kids, to any old problem. It changed my life, plain and simple. For a masterclass in the R Factor, I encourage you to read one of the most impactful books I have ever read: *Man's Search for Meaning* by Victor E. Frankl.

THE LESSON: YOU CONTROL YOUR RESPONSE!

You don't control events, or even their outcomes. You just control your response, but that's honestly everything!

Here's a story I love to tell. Once while I was away on a trip, I called home to check in. Steph answered the phone in a really rough, upset manner: "Hello??"

Caring husband that I am, I immediately asked, "What's wrong?"

She said (in a not-so-nice tone), "Your son didn't put the cap on the hot sauce, and when I opened the fridge, it busted all over the floor."

She was frustrated—rightfully so—and started to blame and complain a little. But then I heard her pause. The next thing out of her mouth was, "Well, these floors needed cleaning anyway, so it's a great opportunity to get that done." Whew! What an awesome lens to see the situation through!

Stephanie took a reflective pause: a short pause after the event when you take a breath and think. Even though her pause was after the fact, I knew she was making progress with her thoughts!

She was able to take that breath, and that's all that needed to happen to get her mind right and change the whole story. She resisted that urge to blame and complain, and thank goodness, because I can testify that an impulsive negative response is very unbecoming, and has never solved a problem or added value to any situation. I have learned that if I can respond to issues above the line and with intention, others around me start to do the same thing. It is a better way to live!

That's E + R = O in real life.

Another great example is the way I used to respond when quarterbacks threw interceptions or running backs fumbled. Ten years ago, I absolutely blasted the quarterback (LD, KP, Frank, y'all know what I am talking about). The thing is, everyone in the entire stadium saw the player's mistake, and my reaction only made it worse.

Let's use E + R = O with that kind of situation. The event is the interception. The outcome we want is . . . well, *no* interceptions. The below-the-line response (impulsive, on autopilot, resistant) is to bring more attention to the situation by yelling and placing blame on the quarterback. The outcome of *that* kind of response is going to be a player who is timid and scared to make a throw when he goes back out—a worse football player than he was before.

An above-the-line response (intentional, on purpose, skillful) would be to get curious. What did you see? What was your thinking? How can we prevent this from happening again? This puts a more educated quarterback back on the field and gets us closer to the response we want to have, which is a confident quarterback capable of playing his best when his best is needed. The goal is to become more curious than furious.

How you respond is always a choice. Sure, you can always blame the players (remember chapter 1), blame the officials, blame the weather, or ignore other people's advice. But nothing of value ever comes from that kind of attitude or response. The better way forward is to stop, reflect, and get curious: What went well? What went wrong? What can we do better next time? *How can we learn from this?* That's where growth happens. That's where improvement lies! Pause, get your mind right, and take the best action to influence the best response possible.

The difference between a good team and a great team (or a good *you* and a great *you*) often comes down to the ability to pause, own the response, and choose growth over emotion. Take control of your thoughts and be the boss of your emotions. When you pause, you give your mind the opportunity to find a better response that can increase your chances of a more productive outcome.

THE CHALLENGE: WELL–BETTER–HOW

At the end of each day, take a few minutes to reflect using this simple framework:

- What did I do **well** today? List three.
- What can I do **better** next time? List two.
- **How** am I going to be better next time? List one.

Focus your answers and reflections here on your E + R = O moments that didn't go quite right, when you didn't react how you feel you should have. Write it down. Without reflecting on the things to which we didn't respond well, we repeat negative cycles. When we reflect on R's that were less than, and decide a better response, we increase our odds of responding better next time.

Maybe your kid spilled a glass of milk, and you hollered at them, so that night, you write about it. Ask yourself, "How could I have responded better? How am I going to prepare to make it happen differently next time?" That's how growth happens, just one deliberate response at a time.

Event + Response = Outcome. You can't control the E. You can't always predict the O. But you can always own your R! The better your R, the more the opportunity to influence the O.

NO BCD

E + R = O starts with no blaming, complaining, and/or getting defensive (BCD). You cannot kick-start E + R = O while doing this! So, step number one is to eliminate all BCD from your life.

If there's one thing I've learned over the years, it's that *nothing* good ever comes from blaming, complaining, or being defensive. Nothing. Zero! Brian and Tim Kight are the ones who taught me to call it BCD, and they also taught me that it's one of the most destructive habits a leader, coach, or *anyone* can have.

Complaining is like showing up to a party when you're sick. You arrive, gather together with all your friends, and then (of course) you all wind up going home sick at the end of the night! Complaining, blaming, and getting defensive . . . it's contagious. Before you know it, everyone around you catches your bad habits. Again, BCD serves no purpose! Maybe it makes you feel a little better in the moment—you get that satisfaction from letting off some steam—but at the end of the day, *you're still sick*, and you've made it all the worse by bringing others down as well.

Let's role-play. I'm the therapist, and you are my client. You're engaged, and you come in to see me for some premarriage counseling before the big day. As we talk, I give you this advice: After you're married, blame your spouse for everything that goes wrong. Complain about everything he or she does. If your spouse ever tries to give *you* any advice, get very defensive about it.

How do you think your relationship would go? Probably not very well. How many marriages are run that way, even though it's not so explicitly stated as a rule? What's the divorce rate in this country? Google it . . . it's high and only climbing higher!

BCD has never solved a problem, made a relationship better, or added value to anyone's life. It shifts the focus from fixing a problem to making it worse, or (at best) to living in the problem longer. You are either contributing to the solution or reinforcing the problem. There is no middle ground.

Let's try to understand BCD a little bit more.

Why do we BCD? It is a kind of emotional protection. It's our way of shielding our precious egos from harm. It is a form of victim mentality, which many walk through life with.

And more than anything, I believe it stems from a lack of self-awareness. We do not even realize we are doing it. It just comes naturally to us.

We must first become *aware* before we can hope to fix anything. Once we're aware, then *how* do we begin to fix this natural problem? The first thing we must do is take complete ownership of our life.

We need to shift our mindsets: Life is not happening *to* us; it is happening *for* us. Both the good and bad alike are lessons to make us grow and become better. We have to be aware that we can't learn, grow, or get better while making excuses and BCDing!

Second, we need to trade *being frustrated* for *becoming fascinated*. We need to become curious beings. We need to ask, in any and every circumstance, "What can I learn from this?" This solves many issues.

And finally, we just need to shift the lens from *victim* to *problem solver*. When something is not going right, fix it! Find *solutions* instead of *excuses*. Both options are available to us every day and every moment. You will find whatever you choose to look for, both the good and the bad. Where your focus goes, so shall your life grow.

Okay, so now that we understand what BCD is and how we can minimize it in ourselves, the question becomes: How can I get *others* to stop doing it too?

I remember calling Brian one day, asking him how on earth I could teach my wonderful, short-fused wife to pause before BCDing. I wanted her to get control of that R Factor in the E + R = O equation and reject BCD. He just laughed and said, "John, maybe you should focus on being the pause yourself."

He was right. I needed to just do what I was trying to teach, focus on my own R Factor and my own tendency to BCD, and not worry about the rest. I needed to *become* the calm, model that steady, controlled response, instead of just talking about it or wishing other people would do it.

That simple phrase—*be the pause*—changed things for me. It's one thing to know the equation, E + R = O, but it's another thing entirely to live it out, especially when emotions are running high. When you choose to pause instead of blaming, to stay grateful instead of complaining, and to listen instead of defending, you take away the power of negativity. You become the example instead of adding to the problem.

You cannot change other humans. Other humans must *want* to change. What I have found is that if I can be the change and be an example worth catching, others will want to change and do the work. My wife, that same short-fused woman, has a much longer fuse now than she used to. She grew her wick! She saw, she liked, she changed. Life is always an opportunity to get better! We are living it! If you know someone who lives the BCD life, *you* make the change. You show them the way. If they like what they see, they too may change.

BCD destroys relationships, kills teams, and makes you sick. But the opposite—owning your response, solving problems, building relationships, and getting better—that's where life happens. That's leadership. We are always getting better or getting worse. It is a choice!

Let's look at a few examples of commonplace BCD. Call 'em case studies, if you like.

We'll start with traffic.

How many times have you been stuck in traffic and become annoyed? Let me answer for the masses: many, many times! Now, did your annoyance cause the traffic to move along faster? Did it speed it up in any way? Of course not.

A better way of looking at traffic is using the pre-pause. Take a moment to really understand, before you even get into the car, that traffic may occur. It has nothing to do with you; it just is what it is. Traffic happens.

With the pre-pause, you say to yourself, "I will enjoy the scenery on my trip today. If I end up in traffic, it will be a great opportunity to listen to more of my book or podcast, or to call a friend and check in."

There are plenty of options. It all starts with No BCD, and with changing the story you are telling yourself. *You cannot be hateful and grateful at the same time.*

I have also used the pre-pause to prepare for the eventuality of someone cutting me off in traffic. Instead of getting angry, which makes my driving worse, I have a pre-planned story I tell myself, "I bet they are in a hurry to see their loved one in the hospital." That little story always changes the game! My blood pressure stays down, my driving skills stay up, and after all, who knows where they're going? It could totally be true. No BCD! *Solve problems by creating stories that serve you.*

Now, let's look at the BCD that you might engage in at the airport (a real breeding ground for BCD). For this one I've got a specific, real-life example: One time, Stephanie and I were in Orlando, Florida, catching a 5 a.m. flight back to Pearl, Mississippi. The early flight would get us home in time for work on a Monday morning.

The night before, we got an email that the flight had been delayed until 10 a.m., which meant we were going to have to call in and take the day off—the exact situation we were trying to avoid (hence the 5 a.m. flight!).

I was all in on the R Factor at this point in time, but Stephanie was not. So, when the email came through, it frustrated us both for a minute. I quickly reframed it with some very positive thoughts, like:

"We don't control the flights, so not much we can do."

"At least we don't have to wake up so early tomorrow."

"We will get an extra day off, so that's not so bad. Who doesn't like a four-day week!"

Meanwhile, Stephanie was as mad as a hornet, just very, very aggravated and doing her fair share of BCDing. Guess what? We were not asked by the airline if the change was okay with us! We did not get to select the time we rescheduled it for! They didn't even ask for our opinion about the whole thing! How dare they?

What we *did* get was an extra day off, a chance to sleep in a bit, a great breakfast, and a little more time together. What a blessing!

Let's look at one final example, this time from the gridiron.

Prior to the No BCD Policy we adopted, I would make a list at the end of each season and go to the principal's office to give him a rundown of all the reasons we could not win a state championship at Pearl High School. I could come up with an awful lot of reasons, *none of which had anything to do with me.*

Sound familiar? If you have not had a behavior skills training course, my guess is this may be what you do as well.

After R Factor training and implementing the No BCD Policy, though, excuses were off the table. It was now time for the mirror test. Time to look at the man in the mirror and find answers to issues instead of shining a spotlight on them and then doing nothing about them. From that point forward, if a problem presented itself, we tried to invent or find an answer. If it was a behavior issue with a player, we created a lesson to teach him that missing skill. If it was something we needed funds for, we raised the money. Whatever it was, we looked for an answer. Excuses were gone.

Have I told you we went on to play for *four* state championships after that turning point? Eliminate BCD from your life and watch your life take off like a rocket! #NSGB

THE LESSON: STOP THE SPREAD! ELIMINATE IT FROM YOUR LIFE!

Every time we blame, complain, or get defensive, we destroy relationships. If you want to change your team, your marriage, your family culture? Start by cutting out BCD. It's that simple. If you don't feed it, it'll die. Instead of giving in to that negativity, solve problems! Build relationships! Never Stop Getting Better!

The ultimate lesson any of us could stand to learn comes from the late Tim Kight. When his close friend and doctor came in and delivered him some horrible, horrible news—Stage IV, incurable cancer—Tim replied with, "It is an honor to be chosen. I have worked for this my whole life: It's E + R = O time, Doc! Tell me what to do, and let's get to work."[10] (See the *Never Stop Getting Better* podcast, Episode 28, "USC Trojans Leadership Coach Tim Kight Delivers a Masterclass on the 'R' Factor.")

Wow. Even with the worst of the worst diagnoses, Tim was saying, "What good does adding negativity do, for us or for the people in our life?"

Every decision you make is a step toward becoming the person you want to be. How do you want to show up for others?

Never Stop Getting Better!

THE CHALLENGE: TWENTY-FOUR HOURS BCD-FREE

The challenge for this chapter is a (seemingly) simple one. Don't blame, complain, or get defensive for twenty-four hours . . . I dare ya. Try it!

Now, I fully expect you to fail at this challenge several times before you actually succeed at it. That's fine. We all fail at first. Each day, reflect on how things went down, and then give it a go again the next morning. I might even suggest wearing a rubber band on your wrist, and every time you catch yourself in BCD, give it a little snap as a reminder to pause and reset your response. Because yeah: You control your response, and that's it—and that's everything!

No BCD. Just DMGB: Doesn't Matter, Get Better. Never Stop Getting Better.

CHAPTER 5

SUCCESS VS. SIGNIFICANCE

IT WAS THE end of July 2014, the Tuesday before fall camp was due to start. We were a top-ten team in the state of Mississippi that year, and the season looked like it was going to be a great one. We were prepping for our first big team meeting, and my wife headed off to do registration at a nearby elementary school. My daughter, Haley, went along with her—she was about to be a junior in high school and was one of our team managers at the time.

Well, at about ten o'clock that morning I got a call from Stephanie, and she delivered the completely unexpected news that Haley had just had a seizure. A *seizure*, really?? Nothing like this had ever happened before! I rushed to join them at the elementary school, and we all headed off to the emergency room (ER). My mind was buzzing with the shock and worry of it all. On the way to the ER, we called my parents, who were both nurses. They recommended that we head to a different hospital, so we did.

We sat in the ER for around twelve hours that day. Haley proceeded to have two more seizures, and we were as scared as we had ever been.

The doctors tried to discharge her with instructions to follow up with our pediatrician, but Stephanie refused. She was adamant that someone was going to do *something* that night, because we were not taking our child home to die in front of us!

After three days of tests, Haley was diagnosed with an autoimmune disease called postural orthostatic tachycardia syndrome, or POTS. There is no cure for POTS, and there's really no treatment for it either. All you can do is target the symptoms and do a lot of praying. About half of the people with POTS outgrow it, and the other half are left to suffer terrible symptoms such as fainting, seizures, extreme fatigue, gastrointestinal issues, and plenty more.

In the months that followed, our family's life completely turned on its head. Haley had seizures every single day for the next eight months. Many days, she experienced *multiple* seizures. We had to move her mattress to the ground so she wouldn't fall out of bed in the night, and we even had to sit with her in the bathroom while she showered in case a seizure struck, causing her to fall and hit her head.

She was being treated by the premier POTS doctor, and he had her on up to twenty-eight pills, many of them supplements, daily. Stephanie took her to a treatment center in Dallas for two weeks because we had heard good things about the work they were doing there. It was one of those things that you had to "buy into," and Haley did not; she thought it was nothing more than voodoo. The doctors at the treatment center suggested we pull her out of school and homeschool her, but she was adamant that would not happen. Our doctor agreed to let her stay in school with the understanding that, when she had a seizure, she would rest for a short while in the nurse's office and then return to class only if she was able.

During this difficult and overwhelming time, we struggled with daily life, so extended family moved in to help us take care of things. I'd go to work every day and just wait for the call to come in, telling me that Haley'd had a seizure in class and needed to be picked up from school. On the days she stayed home with her grandparents, Haley would call Stephanie crying and begging her to come home. It was absolutely miserable, and it was absolutely unceasing. There is no worse suffering in the world than when your child suffers.

I'm not proud of it, but up until then, my life's priorities had always been structured something like this: Up at the top was football, and football, and football . . . then down at the bottom came my family, and then beneath that, finally, my faith. I was living what David Brooks would label a "Mountain 1" life, one focused on the world's idea of success, things, money, and titles. But Haley's illness started to move me in the direction of "Mountain 2" life, one focused on significance, on family, and on faith.

Now, Brooks's book, *The Second Mountain: The Quest for a Moral Life*, really digs into this idea in depth, and I highly recommend y'all give it a read. He talks about the difference between living a life focused on success (building your résumé) versus one focused on significance and purpose (building your soul), and about how you must walk into the deep, dark valley in order to transition from the first mountain to the second. We have to experience dark to know what light is, suffering to know what joy is, good to know what bad is.

But here's how that idea got lived out in my own world. During those eight months, watching my daughter struggle, feeling my relationship with my wife fraying and my focus on football simply melting away— that was 100 percent my valley. But I came out the other side changed beyond recognition.

To get from one mountain to the other, you have to walk through that valley.

Haley's seizures shifted everything about how I saw the world. Football? Not so important in light of the misery I saw in my daughter's eyes and the incredible pain that came from not being able to help my own hurting child. Sure, I was still leading one of the best teams in the state, and we were winning our games, but I wasn't celebrating as much. After each of those games, all I could think about was whether Haley had had a seizure that day. Win, lose, or draw . . . who really cared? Football wasn't what truly mattered. My family, that's what mattered. And I was learning that was the thing I had absolutely zero control over.

Speaking of family, during that awful time, when all my priorities and my focus were so drastically and necessarily reset, my wife and I were fighting like we had never fought before. (If you're a parent who's been through something like this with your own child, I'm sure that sounds familiar.) We were broken people. Finally, one night after nearly four months of the ordeal, I asked my wife if we could just hold hands and say a prayer. We were completely worn down by it all.

Four months was way longer than we should have waited to pray, but we lay there together and prayed something like, "We can't control this, God. We can't fix this. We need you. Can you help us?"

Now I'd like to say Haley's seizures just miraculously stopped immediately after that, but they didn't. I don't really know what happened, but we definitely got some kind of outside help. For the first time in weeks and weeks and weeks, we both slept peacefully through the night, side by side.

Haley's seizures eventually stopped several months later. Life went back to "normal," but in truth, things were never the same. And praise Jesus! We had turned the reins over to God and admitted that we couldn't handle things on our own. My priorities had been completely broken down and put back together in a new order: faith, family, *then* football. I'd made the long, hard walk to the second mountain.

I still fail daily, of course, but I am very grateful for the struggles in my life. I now know that God allows us to go through the valley so we can become more of what he wants us to be. That valley taught us many lessons that last to this day. Be thankful for the good, the bad, and the ugly! They are but lessons for us to learn, so that we can be who God made us to be.

Here's one last example of what happened as my focus shifted to significance over success. On November 30, on the eve of the 2017 Class 6 State Championship game, our son J had a theater audition . . . and my wife Stephanie was busy with a school-related activity. On that pivotal night, the night before the *biggest* game of my career, there I was, sitting in a theater and watching auditions for hours.

Now this may seem like a very normal thing to you—exactly what you'd expect of any father in my position—but for me, having lived with the priorities I'd lived with for so long? It was a huge moment. It was proof that change was occurring. I am not proud to say it, but in the years before Haley's seizures, I would have absolutely balked at this notion. The night before the biggest of big games, you want me to do *what*? I would have thrown a fit, because in my mind, it would have been all about me.

But on that particular day, I was able to sit there and feel proud, watching J do what he does. Years later, J recalled this very event to me with these words: "Dad, it meant so much to me that on the eve of your biggest game *ever*, you were in a place I know you didn't really want to be . . . for me."

This is significant. You know, I am not proud of who I was then, but I am proud of who I am becoming. The Never Stop Getting Better journey is about consistently becoming the best version of yourself.

THE LESSON: RESET YOUR PRIORITIES

I started coaching differently after that experience with Haley's seizures. I began to care more about the kids' hearts and character than just their performance. Ironically, when I did that, we started winning even more.

In 2017, we won the state championship. For a high school coach, that's the pinnacle, the very tippy top of the mountain. *You've made it.* But the next morning, you wake up, and you're asking, "What's for breakfast?" You're already looking for what's next. The mountaintop doesn't fill you up like you think it will.

Sylvester Stallone said in a documentary that after creating *Rocky*, after fighting to sell it and finally hitting it big, he got to the top of the mountain and said, "I'm lonely. It's not what I thought it would be."[11]

That's it right there. Chasing the wrong things will never satisfy you. Success will never fill the hole that only significance can.

We only live once on this earth. And when we're lying on our death-bed, we won't be thinking about championships. We'll be thinking about family, friends, faith, and whether we loved people well. That's the second mountain. That's where significance lives.

I spent the first part of my life climbing the wrong mountain. It looked good. It felt good. People clapped for me. But when I got to the top, I realized it wasn't what I thought it would be.

The valley—Haley's illness, the fear, the helplessness—that's what moved me from Mountain 1 to Mountain 2. From chasing things to chasing purpose.

So, what about you? Are your priorities out of whack? Are you chasing things that don't matter? Do you know the difference between success and significance? This is your chance to define those things properly, categorize them accordingly, and make sure you're doing what God calls you to do: living out your purpose. God is working all things together for good, and you were put on this earth for a reason. So act like it!

THE CHALLENGE: CHECK YOUR MOUNTAIN

Here's your challenge for this chapter: Do a "mountain check."

Grab a sheet of paper and make two columns. Label one "Mountain 1: Success." Label the other "Mountain 2: Significance."

Now take an honest look at your life. Where's your time going? Where's your money going? Where's your energy going?

List it all out. Then take a good hard look at the evidence and ask yourself:

Which mountain am I really climbing?

What is success to me—how much I make, or how I show up for others?

If you're not sure where you are, look at your calendar and your checkbook. They'll tell you exactly what you value most.

It's never too late to switch mountains. You just have to be willing to walk through the valley.

PART 2

BUILD THE
HABITS

CHAPTER 6

DON'T QUIT, CAN'T FAIL

VINCE LOMBARDI IS commonly credited with saying, "Winners never quit, and quitters never win." How true is that?

Our team had a 16–0 state championship run in 2017, and we were only the third team in Mississippi history to accomplish that. But it almost never happened. Heck, my move to Nixa and winning the Central Ozark Conference, playing for back-to-back Class 6 state championships, almost never happened. A whole ton of stuff would have never come to be, if my dad chose, just once, to say, "Okay son, come on home." Let me explain.

Way back in the fall of 1989, I began my college football career at Hinds Community College (HCC) in Raymond, Mississippi. Hinds is *the* junior college for the area I grew up in, and back then you were constrained to go to the one in your district, so that's where I went. I was fortunate enough to get a half-scholarship offer, too, so I was excited about that. As a five-foot-ten offensive lineman, no one was really knocking my door down for my services. I grew up very modestly, with two awesome parents who held classic working-middle-class jobs.

Going to college without any scholarship assistance would have been difficult. Doable, but difficult.

We were about two weeks into the most hellish practice schedule you could ever imagine. At the time, you could have what was called "three-a-days." You young people have no idea what this was like. "Three-a-days" means just that: We would legitimately condition and practice three full times each day! The coaches at Hinds probably brought in over one hundred players, and I am convinced that the plan was to run off half of them through those hardcore practices. There was no shortage of midnight runs (which is what we called it when a player quit and just disappeared in the middle of the night, never to return). I validated this theory years later while coaching at Northeast Mississippi Junior College in Booneville, Mississippi. We definitely had the midnight runners.

Coach Gene Murphy (172–76–5, six state championships) is one of the most successful coaches in Mississippi junior college football history. He is small in stature, but boy, was he tough on us. I did not particularly care for him much at that time, if I'm completely honest. He had a very high standard of operation, and I did not. I was a homesick momma's boy, although I was only forty-five minutes from home. Plus, my girlfriend of four years had just broken up with me, and I wasn't sure I would ever find another one. (I bet you can remember being young and having similar thoughts!) I was simply *not having fun*, and I was not at all sure that this was where I wanted to be.

Now, I had a great friend from Pearl High School who had also signed on to play at HCC. He had an outstanding career at Pearl, and Hinds was looking for him to come in and contribute right away (not so the case with me). They expected a lot from him. Coach Murphy was very tough on him, though looking back now, I can't say he was particularly tougher on my friend than he was on everyone else. Coach Murphy was just tough in general. The true definition of a hard-nosed coach!

Regardless, eventually the day came when my friend decided to take action. He took his key to Coach Murphy and turned it in so he could quit and go home. Then he went back to his dorm room and called his dad to let him know his decision. His dad just replied, "Come on home, son." Just like that, he was done. He wasn't the only one either. After two weeks, we were probably having to call some players back to keep the roster at fifty-five. Coach Murphy was *tough*. (Have I told you that yet?)

Well, for someone like me who was really struggling, all that quitting started to seem like a fantastic idea. We all know quitters gather in circles. Well, I went to the next practice or two after my friend left, then decided I was going to do the same. I pranced up to Coach Gene Murphy's office with some newfound courage, gave him some lame excuses for why I had to quit, and turned in my key. Then it came time to call my dad with the news, just like my friend had done. But the conversation didn't go the same way for me. Not at all.

"Dad," I said, "I've decided to quit. I just don't like it anymore."

There was a pause.

"John," he replied, "you can quit if you want to, but you'll have to find somewhere else to live. If you quit, you can't live here." *Click.*

I sat there stunned, wondering where I'd gone wrong. Didn't my dad love me? My emotions were swirling, but I knew one thing for sure: He was serious. I could not go running home.

I sat down on my bed and contemplated my next move. With no other family anywhere close by and no better options I could think of, I landed on taking a return trip to Coach Murphy's office.

I was scared to death on that walk back to face the tough man. *Will he give me the key back? Probably not. Where will I go if he refuses?* All the negative thoughts were just flooding in.

I told Coach Murphy I'd made a mistake and didn't want to quit after all, and I timidly asked for my key back. Lo and behold, he graciously allowed me to continue playing football at HCC—again, one of the premier junior college football programs in the country at the time. (It occurs to me now, this was probably not the first time something like this had happened to him.)

From that day forward, I had a totally different outlook on college football, "three-a-days," and life in general. Perspective matters! I was extremely grateful to have a room and a bed to sleep in, as well as a team to belong to. To this very day, I am so grateful that Coach Murphy allowed me to stay on and learn the many valuable lessons that the great sport of football teaches.

I went on to be an all-state offensive lineman as a sophomore, transferred to Harding University and became an all-conference offensive lineman, met the wife of my dreams, stepped into the coaching profession that I love, and have an all-around *outstanding* life. None of this would have happened if my dad had just said, "Okay son, come on home." He taught me what tough love really is that day. I owe my career to the man, and I tell him so often, with a big ol' thank-you for *not allowing me to quit.*

I must also add, both tough-as-nails Coach Gene *and* his wife, Dot Murphy (the first female football coach in America, who coached wide receivers and kickers), were outstanding Christian leaders. Sometimes God blesses you with incredible mentors, and you are too dumb to actually realize it and be grateful for it at the time. Thank you, God!

THE LESSON: NEVER QUIT

If you don't quit, you can't fail! Say it with me: Don't quit, can't fail! Don't quit, can't fail! Don't quit, can't fail! So . . . just don't ever quit. Just keep on chopping.

And if you're finding yourself fighting the urge to give up, ask yourself: Who are the people you can lean on? Who'll push you to keep on fighting, no matter what? Find them. Ask them to hold you accountable. Sometimes we need tough love, like I did from my dad that day, even though I had no idea what an impact that conversation would have on my life.

You won't reap the rewards if you let yourself give up, which is all the more likely to happen if you don't surround yourself with people who push you to keep moving forward. Remember, anything great will not be easy, and anything easy will not be great! Make a deal with yourself the next time something gets hard: *You will not quit.* No matter what! Just repeat the chant: Don't quit, can't fail! Don't quit, can't fail!

THE CHALLENGE: SEVEN-DAY "GET IT DONE" COMMITMENT

We've all got things we procrastinate or things we're constantly on the edge of quitting. What's one of yours? Pick something fairly small and reasonably achievable this time around. Maybe it's just cleaning out your closet or your car, finally reading that one book a friend recommended, starting an exercise regimen, or teaching your stubbornly scared kid to ride a bike.

Do you have your thing in mind? Schedule it. You've got seven days to make it happen. *No matter what,* do it for the full seven days! Go get 'em. Start it and finish it without quitting. It'll be worth it, I promise.

CHAPTER 7

THE BEST THREE REP MAX OF THE DAY

MY WIFE USED to have about a zillion alarms set each morning, all set just a few minutes apart, because she knew she was going to hit snooze the first few times an alarm went off. She *planned* on it, really, and it drove me absolutely nuts.

The thing is, when you hit the snooze button, your brain actually starts another sleep cycle. Studies show that if you fall back asleep, even just for a few minutes, your body releases chemicals that put you back into rest mode.[12] So when you *do* finally drag yourself out of bed, you're stuck feeling groggy, foggy, and behind. It can take hours for your brain to fully reset from that.

Getting up at the first alarm is like your first rep of the day. It's your first test of discipline, and it's a small but powerful way to win the morning before the rest of the world even wakes up.

For me, consistently getting up at 5 a.m. each day to do some early morning reading and/or a walk with my bride has become essential and sacred. It's quiet. No phone buzzing. Just time to read, pray, think, and prepare. That rhythm gives me a head start mentally, physically, and spiritually. Winning the morning sets a positive day in motion!

Stephanie and I have gotten into the routine of waking up early, taking a thirty-minute walk, listening to a podcast, and praying together. All these actions put together set us up for a great day. Think about it: Before most people get out of bed, we have walked one and a half miles, put some great info into our mind, gotten some fresh air, and prayed! What a blessing that we get to do so *together*.

I began my practice of waking at 5 a.m. and reading for thirty minutes about fifteen years ago (or was it eighteen years ago? It's hard to nail down the exact time!) That routine has only deepened and expanded since then. On many mornings I read for at least an hour, and I can read for up to three hours on Saturdays and Sundays. The compound interest of reading daily for years has shown up in many ways, especially through opportunities to deliver keynote speeches; to teach mental fitness training to individuals, teams, and business; and to teach leadership to organizations. (And have I mentioned, it's also helped us win more football games?)

Making a habit of absorbing information leads to more knowledge in general, as well as an ever-growing list of stories I can share with our team. And we all know we learn more from stories than lectures.

THE LESSON: SNOOZERS ARE LOSERS

Getting up early is a kick start to daily life. Don't just take my word for it, research backs it up! Most high performers and top leaders are early risers. They use those quiet hours to set the tone for the day before the world starts making demands of them.

Here's the lesson: You've got about eighteen seconds when the alarm goes off before your brain talks you into going back to sleep.[13] That's your window to win. So you have eighteen seconds to get your (1) butt off the bed, (2) feet on the floor, and (3) body in the shower. Hence: the best three rep max (3RM) in the world. (Okay, so my three rep max may actually be [1] butt off the bed, [2] feet on the floor, and [3] coffee cup full and book in hand! The point is, you've got eighteen seconds to get up!)

If you snooze, you lose—literally. How you do the first thing in the day often predicts how you'll do everything else. Start by procrastinating, and guess how the rest of the day is going to play out? But start the day with discipline, and you'll build momentum. I say, let's start the day by going 1–0 and then start building more wins from there.

They say integrity is keeping the promises you make to yourself. If this is true and you set the alarm for 5 a.m. but choose to hit the snooze button three times, then your integrity is taking a hit. You are 0–3 to start the day. How you do *anything* is how you do *everything*. Little things add up to big things. Have I gotten my point across yet??

Get up when you say you're gonna get up! And get up earlier than others do. Win the day by winning the morning! Let's goooooo!

I use the three rep max as a way to teach our kids how to be efficient with their time. This is the exact, word-for-word lesson I share with our team. (Thank you to Chris Yeager of Mountain Brook Football for contributing to this story!)

WINNERS AND THEIR SUMMER WORKOUTS: 3RM

With summer workouts beginning Monday morning, it's a good time to discuss two types of people: 1) Average Andy and 2) Winner Willie. Let me explain what I mean and how both athletes get themselves to workouts.

AVERAGE ANDY:

Saturday: No thoughts of summer workouts

Sunday: Stray thoughts of, "Dang, summer workouts start tomorrow. I have to be there at 7:30 a.m.! I can leave at 7:20 and make it. I'll wake up at 7:15."

Monday: Thinks, "It's summertime, why am I even doing this?" as he hits the snooze button, dreading getting out of bed. Finally rolls out of bed, puts clothes on and stumbles out of the house, and arrives late, claiming, "I ain't late!" Is that success? Not even close!

WINNER WILLIE:

Saturday: Already thinking about Monday's workout, anticipating getting the summer started and somewhat excited to show up and improve. A little concerned about what the team will be doing, what time he will need to get there, what time he will have to get up.

Sunday: Thinks about Monday's workout. Coach's words ring in his mind. "To be early is to be on time, to be on time is to be late, and to be late is, well . . . terrible." Makes a plan to be early.

I want to be in the field house at 7:15 a.m.

I live ten minutes away, so I will leave at 6:55 a.m. to account for bad traffic, car problems, and walking to the field house from my parking spot . . .

I will need to eat breakfast at 6:30 a.m. because I know my body needs the fuel.

I will set my alarm for 6:00 a.m., and when it goes off, I know I have eighteen seconds to:

1. Get my butt off the bed
2. Put my feet on the floor
3. Get my body in the shower

If I hit the snooze button, I am a loser. Coach says, "Snoozers are losers!"—and I am no loser!

This is the best 3RM of the day! This plan gives me plenty of time to take care of my business, have a winning start to my day, and be the best that I can be.

Monday: ACTION. DO IT! It's already been done in my mind twenty times, so knock it out! Winners win! Losers lose! I will start my day with the 3RM of winners!

THE CHALLENGE: BE AN EARLY BIRD

For the next week, wake up just fifteen minutes earlier than you usually do. Use that time for one simple task, or maybe to do something intentional: a short workout, reading, prayer, journaling, or planning your day. Pick something you like to do and do it!

Then ask yourself, how does it feel to start the day ahead instead of behind?

Get up at alarm number one. Don't snooze on your goals. Remember: Snoozers are losers, and you are no loser!

CHAPTER 8

STEADY WORK PAYS OFF

MY 2017 FOOTBALL season was supposed to be a good one. We were coming off a 2016 State Championship run that saw us come up a bit short, losing to Clinton 49–35. (I still say, if they hadn't had Cam Akers, we'd have won that game . . . but maybe that's BCDing.)

All our practice gear for 2017 had the number 121 printed on the back. No one knew what the number meant except for our team: It was the date of the 2017 State Championship game, December 1 (or 12/1), in Oxford, Mississippi. We wanted the daily reminder of our goal!

Our task in 2017 was to show up every day to get better. We had a lot of returning players and were ranked preseason number one, so the goal of getting better daily without letting our egos get in the way (or reading our press clippings) was certainly going to be a challenge. Chasing Excellence, as I now call it, was our goal. *Can we wake up every single day, singularly focused on getting better and doing the work?* That was the focus.

We got off to a good start, but not a great start. I believe we were thinking too much of ourselves early on in the season. We had a seven-point win over Warren Central, a ten-point win over Northwest Rankin, and then a week five, seven-point win over Madison Central. To this day, I believe we were outplayed in that game, but we found a way to win it in spite of it. They say most games come down to four or five plays, and I guess we won the majority of them. I do believe that sometimes you learn more from a loss than from any win, and the Madison game was handled like a loss for us. We checked ourselves and decided to put our heads down and go to work. Regardless of what anyone wrote or said about us, we were going to do the work one day at a time, 1 percent at a time!

Over the next nine weeks, our average margin of victory was 43–8. What we learned was how to work regardless of what we thought, felt, or were being told by anyone else. There is a great book that we had used previously as a book study, *Chop Wood Carry Water* by Joshua Medcalf. The moral of the story is that the main character, a young archer, wants to learn to shoot arrows, but the wise sensei puts him through a long series of lessons and tells him, "You must chop wood and carry water daily first."

You cannot place the outcome of what you want in front of the work. The work has to be done before anything great is going to happen. Greatness in any line of work is not achieved by luck. Sure, it is possible to win the lottery, but the large majority of lottery winners end up going broke and being worse off after winning because they didn't have the skills to obtain the money on their own, and they certainly don't have the skills to manage it. There is no shortcut to chasing excellence. It starts with waking up every day (early!) and doing the work. Little things compound into big things.

That's the key to remember: Even if the end goal doesn't happen right away, you have to keep doing things the right way. The tide will always, eventually, turn. Don't let one bad outcome slow you down or discourage you. Steady work pays off.

One of the hardest things in the world to do is work without seeing the results. Why do you think the average person gives up on their New Year's resolutions before the end of January? Twenty-three percent of people who make New Year's resolutions quit within the first week. Only eight percent last a full month.[14] We have no issue eating a cheeseburger every day and not seeing those results very fast. But after several months, we say, "Dang, what is going on? Somehow, I gained weight!" You must be willing to do the work regardless of what you see and feel immediately. It will pay off! You must believe!

THE LESSON: JUST KEEP WORKING!

When things don't go your way, you get to choose whether you're going to panic, or if you're going to persist. In 2017, our team chose to persist, and later on we wound up with a record of 16–0, only the third team in Mississippi history to accomplish this feat. We showed up each day and did the work. Tuned out all media hype—the "rat poison," as Nick Saban would call it.

All you have to do is dedicate yourself to getting 1 percent better each day. Small things turn into big things. How you do anything is how you do everything. Never Stop Getting Better. When we can learn to do the work, no matter what, the outcomes will turn in our favor sooner rather than later. Most will quit too soon. Most do not have the discipline to show up every day to do the work. Your hard work will bear fruit, I swear it.

If *we* managed to accomplish it, you can too. You just have to keep on grinding. Just keep working, no matter how hopeless it seems, and you'll eventually get there. Do the work!

THE CHALLENGE: DON'T FORGET IT

I carry a poker chip, and it never leaves my pocket. It's got "NSGB" stamped on it, alongside "1 percent" and "14:24." Those numbers reference the fact that how you use just 1 percent of your day (fourteen minutes, twenty-four seconds) can make all the difference. It's my physical, daily reminder to never quit, to stay constantly dedicated to getting better.

I want you to create a reminder for yourself too. Maybe it's a special coin, a sticky note, or a key chain. I don't care. Whatever it is, make sure it's something you can keep with you all the time so you can feel it in your pocket every now and again to remember: Steady work pays off. Never Stop Getting Better.

(Not sure what physical reminder to use? Email me at johnperry@ neverstopgettingbetter.net, and you just might have a poker chip show up in the mail one day.)

CHAPTER 9

GARBAGE IN/GARBAGE OUT

EIGHTEEN YEARS AGO, as I've shared, I made the decision to start waking up at 5 a.m. every single day to read for at least thirty minutes. That one choice—to start feeding my mind with something good on the daily—was a big turning point in my personal life and mental fitness. You might even say it's what started my whole Never Stop Getting Better journey! It was one simple decision that was not easy to execute at the time. But I was all in on the commitment to execute this daily. I was motivated!

What I have learned is this: If you squeeze an orange, you are going to get orange juice. You probably wouldn't expect to get grape juice or apple juice, would you? When we are squeezed in life (by adversity), whatever is inside of us will come out. The more quality the inputs, the more quality the outputs, especially in tough times. And tough times are coming to all of us. No one is exempt from going through hard things. You are either just coming out of a hard time, in the middle of a hard time, or a hard time is coming your way. They cannot be avoided.

My 5 a.m. reading habit began at a coaching clinic in Biloxi, Mississippi, when I first heard about the book *Good to Great* by Jim Collins. I'd never really been a reader, but I saw a coach who had been very successful talking about this book and urging the group to read it, so I thought, "If it's good enough for him, I'll give it a shot." I picked it up, and it blew me away. It sparked a desire to *learn more.* They say one match can start a wildfire; well, that book certainly started a wildfire in me.

If you know anything about that book, it looked at companies that started out in similar situations but ended up in very *different* situations. For example: Walgreens became GREAT, while the comparison brand, Eckerd Drugs, went out of business. Kroger became GREAT, while the comparison brand, A&P, went out of business. Why did some become great while others stayed average or went out of business altogether? The common denominator was always the WHO! By this I mean the leadership, and especially the person responsible for being the leader of the team overall. That was the common denominator between the companies that made the leap to GREAT!

I summarized that book's findings in one long sentence, and it's a sentence I have read hundreds of times and shared with many people and businesses since then. It's all about the WHO, and how change starts with *taking ownership*:

> **The best leaders were modest people who constantly asked questions, had the ability to confront the most brutal answers, constantly tried to improve, surrounded themselves with the most-able people, looked at their own mistakes and deficiencies, and were always asking what skills their company would need in the future.**

If we break this all-too-long sentence down, it says that the leaders of the companies that went on to be *great* shared the following behavioral skills: curious, humble, honest, growth-minded, committed to hiring the best, and always striving to get better!

That was my "aha" moment. The book was the mental match I needed to spark a fire and grow my knowledge base, my skills, my understanding of the world, my resilience and persistence, everything. I realized that if I wanted to make others better, *I* had to get better first. I had to start by looking at the person in the mirror. What became crystal clear was that I was, like a large majority of the world, BCDing my life away! Blaming others, complaining about my situation, making excuses for what's not going right, and getting defensive when others tried to help me out with feedback.

Reading became my first step into taking ownership. I started devouring books, podcasts, success hotlines—anything that could sharpen my thinking and help me grow. I started waking up early and reading first thing in the morning. It's still a daily practice, and I still wake up at 5 a.m. each morning (many mornings at 4:30 a.m.) to dig in and stretch my brain. I've also got several degrees from Automobile University at this point, because if I'm driving, you'll catch me listening to podcasts or audiobooks every single time if the drive is fifteen minutes or more. I also started calling the Success Hotline (more to come on this later) around the same time, adding three positive motivational messages a day to my library of thoughts.

Here's a reminder. We have sixty thousand thoughts per day: 90 percent are repetitive, and 80 percent are negative. So, what are we choosing to put into our minds? If it's garbage going in, it'll be garbage coming out. You cannot expect to get apple juice from an orange. Expecting yourself to handle adversity and show up for your loved ones in a crisis when you're putting nothing of value into yourself is pretty fruitless! But if you put in wisdom, perspective, and truth, you will get better thinking, better actions, and better outcomes.

If you want to show up as the best version of yourself for the people you love most, it starts with you. Reading books gives you the opportunity to learn from anyone in the world, living or dead. It gives you an opportunity to learn so much from others, even people you may never meet. My wife and I recently estimated that we have spent between

$25,000–$30,000 on books in the last fifteen years. That's 125 books a year for fifteen years at approximately fifteen dollars apiece. The benefits of this habit have led to the opportunity to host a podcast, win more games, give keynote speeches for businesses and schools, teach leadership to companies, and so much more. To say reading can change your life is absolutely an understatement. After all, what's the difference between those who can't read and those who don't?

Not all readers are leaders, but all leaders are readers.[15]
—**Harry S. Truman**

Reading is essential for those who seek to rise above the ordinary.[16]
—**Jim Rohn**

THE LESSON: WHAT FILLS YOU FORMS YOU

What we put into ourselves shapes everything. You don't get better by accident. You get better by being intentional about what you feed your mind. When asked why they don't read, people normally say, "I am too busy." I do not buy that! What I say is: You are very inefficient with your time. Everyone can manage time better; everyone can find time they are wasting! Cut Netflix off for just fifteen minutes, and you'll see what I mean.

What time do you wake up? Wake up fifteen minutes earlier. If you say you do not have fifteen minutes, you are either lying to yourself or just plain lazy. Either way . . . there *is* time. Most will not do it, I get that. But if you have made it this far in this book, you are the exception, and I know that you have a strong desire to Never Stop Getting Better. So act on it!

Now, I've done the math. Given the average numbers for reading speed and book lengths, if you read for 1 percent (fourteen minutes and twenty-four seconds) of your day, you would be in the top 10 percent of readers in America and the top 5 percent globally.[17] Let me say it again: Just fifteen minutes a day of intentional reading could put you in the top 5 percent of readers on the planet—and give you an unfair advantage in wisdom, language, decision-making, and leadership.

The book *Good to Great* taught me that the best leaders never stop learning. They don't wait to get better; they *choose* to get better! You have to choose to pick up that book, put in those earbuds, and get to listening, reading, growing, and learning.

Even fourteen minutes and twenty-four seconds—just 1 percent of your day—can change your life if you use the time wisely. Read, reflect, and learn for that measly 1 percent of your day; everyone has fourteen minutes and twenty-four seconds to spare in a twenty-four-hour period! If you do it every day, imagine what your mind, your leadership, and your relationships will look like in one year, five years, ten years. Do the work!

THE CHALLENGE: 14:24

For the next thirty days, set aside fourteen minutes and twenty-four seconds (14:24) per day to do something that feeds your growth. Read a book or listen to a podcast that challenges you. The funny thing is, if you commit to doing this for thirty days, I promise you that your 14:24 will increase, because your habit will increase and you will want to read longer. Some people say, "I don't like to read." I say: Read something else. Find something you like and build the habit. If you don't like it, put it down and grab something else. Discipline either works for your good or for your bad. Let it work for your good. Reading is the cheapest and fastest way to borrow someone else's wisdom . . . without borrowing their mistakes.

CHAPTER 10

WALK-ON MENTALITY

AFTER SPENDING TWENTY-FOUR months at Hinds Community College (HCC), where I'd been an all-state offensive lineman, I thought I'd wind up playing at a four-year college next—easy. I quickly came to find out that nobody really wants a five-foot-ten offensive lineman, though. Little did I know at the time how important measurables were in this great game of football, at least to college coaches. And I did not have those measurables. If I am honest, life was also spiraling out of control at this same time due to some very poor life choices I was making, especially related to whom I was choosing to surround myself with.

Despite these barriers, I set my sights on Harding University, a Christian university in Searcy, Arkansas, which was affiliated with the Church of Christ (the type of church I grew up in and where my dad frequently preached). I called up the school, got in touch with the head coach, Larry Richmond, and asked, "Coach, is there any way I can walk on to the team?" He was gracious enough to let me. Little did I *also* know that most Division II schools would be happy to have a practice player who they do not have to put on scholarship.

Now, not a lot of people are begging to walk on a Division II team, not with the $10,000 price tag that comes with it. (In 1991, at least, that was a lot of money.) More than that, walk-ons aren't the best-treated members of the team by any stretch of the imagination. Harding University probably treated walk-ons better than most, but it was still a definite no-thrills experience, as I believe it continues to be today. You might get a shirt . . . or not. You might get a meal . . . or not. You might get a locker . . . or not.

I had to gain the walk-on mentality. I had to be Mr. Humble Pie. I had to tell myself, "It doesn't really matter what the outcome is right now. I'll just work while I wait, do things without praise or glory, and get used to no one really caring if I'm here or not."

Remember, I was First Team All-State, so I thought I was good. Truthfully, I thought I was *owed* a scholarship! My coaches at HCC had assured me I would be receiving offers coming out of the junior college. But nope—not so fast, my friend. Just when you start thinking more of yourself than you should, life has a unique way of throwing you curve balls. I now believe it's God doing what he does to help you be the best you can be for him. He knew I needed to be a walk-on.

I firmly believe that if you aren't getting what you want out of a situation, your failure is due to one of three things: You aren't good enough, you aren't trying hard enough, or you *are* good enough and trying hard enough, but you need to try for *longer*.

Let's apply that to my situation as a walk-on. I had the confidence that I was good enough. (Although as the days ticked by, that confidence was wavering a bit.) Still—number one, check.

Being a walk-on, effort was the name of the game. I worked *hard*. I had been raised by two hard-working humans, so that was just what we did. Number two, check.

I leaned into the truth of number three: I had to keep working hard at it for *long enough*, every day, adding value wherever I could, and eventually I'd see results.

Sure enough, it paid off. I won a scholarship in my second semester (I never could have afforded my college tuition without it!), made the team, and did the thing. I went on to become an all-conference offensive lineman, meet the woman of my dreams, and graduate with honors, all because I stayed humble and learned to work while I waited. (Being a walk-on has added more value to my life than I can describe. Everyone would be better off in life if they had this experience!) I committed to Never Stop Getting Better, no matter the circumstances.

And today I'm out here teaching leadership lessons to Central Bank and many other organizations, getting the opportunity to teach and coach all kinds of groups, and reaping the benefits of daily NSGB.

THE LESSON: BET ON YOURSELF

If you want to move forward, you have to be honest enough to see where you are (the good and the bad of yourself *right now*!) and humble enough to keep wanting to improve. Never Stop Getting Better! The answer is always *Do the work!*

When you hit a wall, it's easy to get frustrated and blame circumstances, luck, or other people. But most of the time, again, it comes down to one of these three truths:

1. You just aren't good enough (yet).
2. You aren't trying hard enough.
3. You're good enough and trying hard enough, but you haven't been doing it long enough.

That framework takes self-awareness. You've got to stop and ask, "What's really holding me back right now?" You can't fix a problem till you name it, and the only thing you have any control over is you—your effort, your attitude, and your ability to keep showing up.

I've seen that principle play out over and over. Take Tyson Lee![18] He was a Division I starting quarterback at Mississippi State, but he began as a walk-on too. I coached him through an all-star game back in 2005, and he's the only kid from that high school team whose name I still remember, even though he was a five-foot-nine quarterback who didn't look like the prototype. Nobody would've bet on him. But he bet on himself. He showed up every single day with great energy, consistent habits, and body language that made people trust him. Eventually, that consistency made him a team captain and starter in the Southeastern Conference.

Or look at Eli Drinkwitz.[19] In 2009, he didn't get the head job at Springdale High in Arkansas. A lot of people would've quit or looked for an easier job. Instead, he stayed on as an assistant, then took a $15,000 quality-control job at Auburn, basically an entry-level grind. He bet on himself, worked, learned, and kept getting better. He didn't even play football in college, but now he's the head coach at Missouri.

Same story with Dan Lanning.[20] He started out working for free as a grad assistant (GA). He and his wife were on EBT benefits just to get by. But he made a decision: If I'm here, I'm going to be the most helpful, hardest-working GA on this team. That attitude built his reputation, and when a paid position opened, he was ready. Fast-forward, he's the head coach at the University of Oregon. Good things happen when you work for them.

All these guys lived out the same truth: If you can't control the outcome, control your input. Keep working. Keep improving. Bet on yourself and create the story you want. Never Stop Getting Better. Whether it takes eighteen months or twenty years, results always come to those who keep showing up and adding value.

THE CHALLENGE: PUT IT ON PAPER

Think of one area in your life that you're frustrated about *right now*. This can be a challenge you're facing as a parent, spouse, football coach, whatever.

Ask yourself honestly, "Why am I not where I want to be with this challenge?"

1. Am I simply not good enough?
2. Am I not trying hard enough?
3. Have I not been trying hard enough (while being good enough) for *long* enough?

Step one is to practice self-awareness. You cannot fix what you are not aware of. Be honest with yourself or ask a friend whom you trust to answer the same questions about you. Write down the thing that's holding you back. Then come up with a plan to target that behavior and track your progress for a week. Do the work!

Putting it on paper is the first step to making it real. Never Stop Getting Better!

Team Perry 2025: J, Stephanie, John, Haley, Georgia

One of the best players ever coached, Tylan Knight,
after a Backyard Brawl win, 2017.

2017 Class 6 State Champions, 16-0

Mom and Dad, Steve and Judy Perry

One of the best players ever coached, 5-star 2025–26 Gatorade National Football Player of the Year Jackson Cantwell, 2025.

Mr. Pearl, Ray Rogers. Pearl's first QB and PA announcer for fifty-six years, a true legend.

My mentors: Bobby Hall and Marcus Boyles

Steph and I after winning the third district championship in a row.

*Steph and I at Harding
University, 1993*

*The love of our life, Georgia, with
her first grape tomato, 2023.*

My dad and J after the 2017 State Championship game.

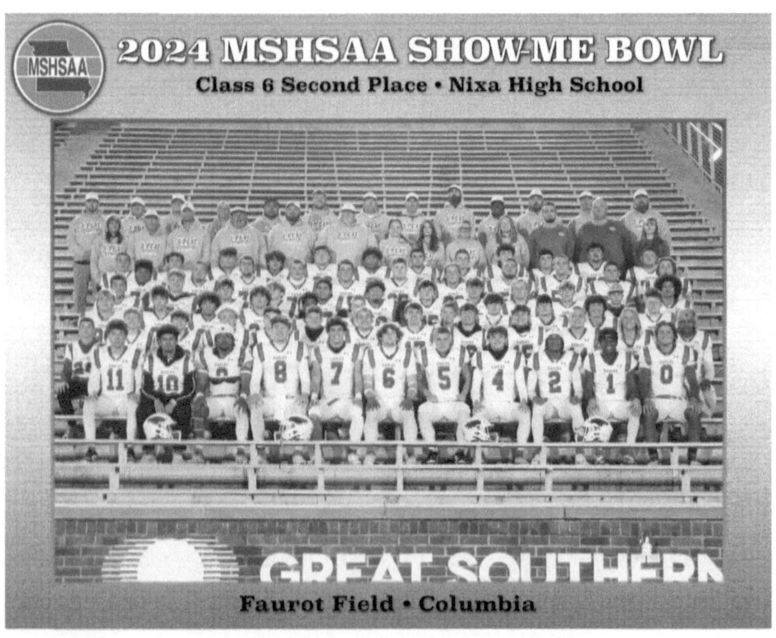

2024 Class 6 State Runner-Up

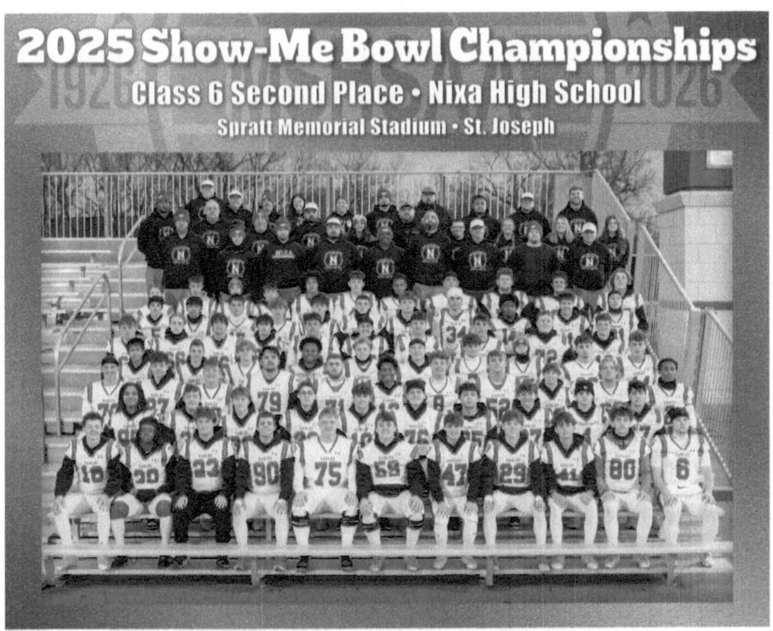

2025 Class 6 State Runner-Up

The reason this book was written, Georgia!

BUILD THE MINDSET

CHAPTER 11

CHASE EXCELLENCE

ONCE HAD the incredible Alan Stein Jr. on the *Never Stop Getting Better* podcast.[21] He's a basketball skills coach and speaker, and he shared one of my favorite stories about the late great Kobe Bryant.

In 2007, Nike decided to host basketball skill camps for young kids. The first-ever Nike Basketball Skills Academy was going to be built around Kobe Bryant. Alan Stein Jr. got invited to help work the camp alongside—you guessed it—the one who started the whole thing, the indomitable Kobe, who, at the time, was the best player on the face of the earth (preceded by Jordan and followed by LeBron).

Alan jumped at the chance, of course, and he took his involvement a step further. He'd heard about the ridiculous individual workouts Kobe put himself through. The first day of camp, after the opening team meeting, Alan asked Kobe if he could come watch one of his personal workouts. Kobe said, "Sure, 4:00 tomorrow." Alan had a curious look on his face because the first session with the kids was at 3:30 p.m. Kobe, seeing his confusion, clarified, "That's 4:00 *a.m.*"

So Alan, wanting to make a great first impression, set his alarm clock for 3:00 a.m. and planned to catch a taxi and arrive before Kobe. When he stepped out of the taxi at 3:30 a.m., he was greeted by the sound of a basketball bouncing and sneakers squeaking on a gym floor. When he entered the gym, Kobe was drenched in sweat. He had already been working for a while.

The first ninety minutes of Kobe's workout contained nothing but the most basic, fundamental drills ever. Alan watched him do the kinds of drills that PE teachers practice with seventh graders, and he was floored. Why was this giant of basketball spending so much time on such elementary skills? He didn't have the nerve to ask about it right away but finally managed it after they'd completed their first skills camp that day. He asked Kobe, "I watched you, the greatest player in the world, practicing the same, most basic skills ever. *Why?*"

And Kobe just gave a little laugh and said, "Why do you think I'm the best player in the world? I *never* get bored of doing the basics!"

Kobe Bryant himself never got bored of drilling the basics. Doing the little things—over and over, to perfection—is what made him great. He woke up every day with the kind of focus that is like looking through a straw, singularly focused on the question: How can I get better today? Just today! Just the little steps. What are the basic fundamentals that I must continue to master? Just achieving excellence in this moment, here and now.

THE LESSON: FOCUS ON TODAY

Never Stop Getting Better is a mindset and a lifestyle. You get up and you decide to be a little better every day, no matter what. It's a relentless pursuit of excellence through mastering the basics. It's a focus on the process over the outcome. That daily discipline and focus on getting better is what makes the difference between people who *do* and those who just *wish* they did.

When it comes to truly pursuing excellence in this way, here's the analogy I like to encourage people to keep in mind:

Think about driving a car. You've got a windshield, rearview mirror, side mirrors, and a GPS (or a navigation app pulled up on your phone). Each one plays a role in helping you get where you're going.

This visual reminds me of how I should look at life on a daily basis. Keep the main thing the main thing.

The windshield represents today—what's right in front of you. It's the biggest window for a reason. When you're driving, you can't see five hundred miles down the road; you can only see what's up ahead *right now*. That's your focus: "I'm gonna Never Stop Getting Better . . . right now. I'm gonna chase excellence *today*." If that means drilling the basics a hundred times, like Kobe, that's what you do. Keep your eyes on where you are going! Take action now. True joy and happiness will always be found in the present moment.

Then you've got your rearview mirror for quick backward-facing checks, so you don't miss out on learning from your past. The rearview mirror helps you see what's behind you. In this analogy, we use the rearview mirror to know where we came from. What are the lessons you need to learn from the past? You are not going to drive out of the rearview mirror. You would not make it very far if you were focused on only the rearview mirror. So, you should not obsess over the past. Learn the lessons you need to learn and get back to the present.

Next, you've got your side mirrors, so you can keep an eye on who's next to you. The people around you are huge influences on you, and they matter, but you don't fix your eyes on those side mirrors or you're sure to crash. Your past and your influences are valuable for context and inspiration and learning, but they aren't your main focus. Because what's your main focus, again? *Today.* How you can be better right now.

Finally, there's your GPS, or your maps app, or whatever. That stands for your vision, your big-picture, overarching goal. You need to set it so you know where you're going. But once your destination is in, you don't sit there staring at the map the whole drive. You check it occasionally to make sure you're still on course, then get your eyes back on the road immediately in front of you. Some people can get lost in daydreaming about the future. Remember: Getting lost in your thoughts, whether the past (rearview mirror) or the future (GPS), can lead to stress, anxiety, etc. True joy and happiness are found in the present. Keep your eyes on the road.

If you want to move forward with purpose, you need all three: awareness of the past, connection with your "ride or dies," clarity about your destination—but your main focus belongs on the present. The road ahead of you today is where excellence actually happens.

THE CHALLENGE: TAKE FIVE

The next time you take a trip to work, school, or the store, take five minutes when you arrive to sit in the car and think about that trip.

Most of the time we do not even think about how we get where we are going. We have subconsciously done it so many times that we just get in and go, and somehow, we arrive safely. But after *this* drive, we want to sit still and ask ourselves a few questions:

- How many times did you check the side mirrors?
- How many times did you check the rearview mirror?
- How much time was spent looking out the windshield?

Do a quick inventory of the time allotted for each item. The next time you have to use your maps to get somewhere, think about how often you looked at the map. This practice is a great reminder that reinforces what's most important: where you are going!

Next, journal about your North Star or big goal (the GPS, in our analogy):

- Who are you surrounding yourself with? (side mirrors)
- What are the things in your immediate past you can use to Never Stop Getting Better? (rearview mirror)
- And most importantly, what are the daily, basic routines you need to be doing every day that will make you excellent at whatever it is you choose to be excellent at?

CHAPTER 12

MENTAL TOUGHNESS

I HAVE A four-second clip from the movie *Rocky* saved on my phone. Bet you can guess which one.

It's that scene when he's taking a heck of a beating and gets knocked down for the zillionth time by the world champion, Apollo Creed. Rocky's manager, Mickey, is telling him to stay down because he is getting killed. But Rocky manages to pick himself up from the canvas one more time to a standing position, then he makes that famous gesture, beckoning his opponent to *bring it on*. The next thing we see is Apollo dropping his head and slumping his shoulders. While he doesn't verbally say anything, his body language says, "Oh crap, I chose the wrong dude to fight! This guy will *never quit*!"—and you probably know the rest of the story. Rocky goes on to lose the fight, but he wins the crowd. (Sometimes we win when we lose.) And then, Rocky comes back in the next fight to win.

That's mental toughness right there! Getting knocked down over and over but always getting up—*that's* thinking like a champion. I've watched that clip hundreds of times. It is a constant reminder that life will knock us down from time to time, but our job is to be tough enough to keep getting up. No matter what! NEVER QUIT!

Back in 1977, the middleweight boxers Eugene "Cyclone" Hart and Vito Antuofermo faced off in the ring. Hart was well known and heavily favored, and he knocked his opponent all around the ring for four rounds. Antuofermo endured the beating so well that he started to tire Hart out! As soon as Hart got discouraged and started to falter, Antuofermo knocked him out with a few swift blows, and that was that. He ended the fight.

When the fight was over, the two fighters were taken back to their respective locker rooms. They were only separated by a thin wall, so each fighter could hear the other speaking. Hart overheard Antuofermo say the following:

> **Every time he hit me with that left hook to the body, I was sure I was going to quit. After the second round, I thought if he hit me there again, I'd quit. I thought the same thing after the fourth round. Then he didn't hit me anymore.**[22]

Hart started crying uncontrollably. What he had learned was that he and Antuofermo had had the exact same thoughts during the fight. The only thing that separated them was Antuofermo did not quit. They both were experiencing the same thing, but one chose to NEVER QUIT!

Antuofermo was mentally and physically tough. He endured and endured, and was able to beat a fighter who was, technically, "better" than him—all because he was willing to put up with the pain longer.

If *you* keep getting up, again and again, you'll win your fair share of fights. Most people quit! So, all you really have to do is endure. Eventually, with enough mental toughness, you can outlast pretty much anything and everyone.

Mental toughness is not just for athletes. It's for the mom raising kids alone, the young man trying to break generational cycles, the student balancing work and school, the employee facing layoffs, and the coach living with the pressure of a whole community's expectations on his shoulders. I know firsthand how mental toughness comes in handy when life throws you a curveball. Life is hard right now, has been hard in the past, or hard times are coming. Mental toughness is required. Do the work!

Mental toughness isn't something you're born with. It's built rep by rep, choice by choice.

THE LESSON: TOO TOUGH FOR THEM, JUST RIGHT FOR US!

That's the way I want to live. That's what I want my teams to play like. That's what I want for *you*: to always, no matter what happens, get up and keep fighting! It truly is a superpower. You have control over your attitude, your effort, and how you approach your "edge." You want to succeed and thrive? Regardless of how you feel, *keep getting up*. That's all you have to do. Most people will quit way before it's time. We live in the most comfortable era in history. You are probably sitting in a cushioned recliner right now, sipping on coffee, getting ready to take a hot shower and then drive to work in a great car. We are in what Michael Easter calls a "comfort crisis" in his book *The Comfort Crisis* (great book by the way). If we just keep getting up, we will win far more battles than we lose. Channel your inner Rocky. If it helps, send me a message, and I will send you the Rocky clip. It works!

We brought Damon West to both Pearl, Mississippi, and Nixa, Missouri, for inspirational purposes. Life is hard and few have experienced the kind of "hard" Damon West did when he received a life sentence in prison. One of the many takeaways from my time with Damon was this: He said, "You do not have to win every fight, you just have to fight every fight." I will never forget that, and I have treasured the friendship we have built.

Tough people win. Pressure is a privilege, and failure doesn't exist: Only learning opportunities do. We win, or we learn! Whatever happens, never quit. Cultivate that growth mindset, accept that things just suck sometimes, don't make excuses for yourself, stay coachable, and learn from your mistakes. *When it's too tough for them, it's just right for us!*

THE CHALLENGE: ONE MORE REP!

The three pillars of mental toughness are effort, attitude, and willingness to tackle your "edge." So here's your challenge: Put in (and track) one more rep for each of those pillars *today*!

For effort, that might look like one more minute in the gym, one more phone call to someone who can help you be better, one more push toward your goal (whatever it may be). Do one more!

For attitude, that might mean you send one additional positive text message today or go out of your way to create one more positive interaction. Reach out to one person and let them know you appreciate what they have meant to you in your life.

When it comes to your edge, it means doing something uncomfortable today. Take a cold shower. Talk to a stranger in the checkout line. Instead of settling into your recliner at the end of a long workday, go take a walk, or clean that mess you left from breakfast. Read a book, listen to a podcast, or watch a motivational YouTube video. Do something you don't wanna do for 14:24!

The next time you get knocked down in life, get up! Keep moving no matter what! Punch back! The mental toughness you build by learning to keep getting up will not only serve you for the rest of your life; it will serve those you lead and surround yourself with! You will be making a difference! Like Nike, "Just do it!"

With each of those three extra reps today, you're building mental toughness galore. Never Stop Getting Better!

CHAPTER 13

CONQUER THE EDGE

KEEP A running list of goals for myself in a Google Doc. Way back in 2019, I added this one: Start a podcast.

I'd been listening to podcasts for a few years at that point, and the urge and conviction to get one of my own going was strong. Not strong enough, though. In the end, it took me a couple of years to actually take even one tiny step toward making it happen. Not because I was ambivalent about the idea—I really, really wanted to start a podcast! But I was too scared to tackle something so new. The inner critic would start with thoughts like, "Who are you to have a podcast? Who would listen? Who would you even interview?" I was avoiding "The Edge." The Edge is that point where things get scary, and you become unsure of whether you can do it. This is a spot where quitting looks like a better decision. We find ourselves at The Edge many times in life.

My wife even bought me a podcast microphone for Christmas in 2020, and I just let it sit there. I was going through the typical feelings everyone feels when they approach their personal edge: self-doubt, fear of failure, imposter syndrome, you name it. I was overrun with negative thoughts. I let those voices creep in and prevent a breakthrough. I let all that junk hold me back for way too long.

In the end, I had to put my money where my mouth was in order to get moving. In May 2023, I finally invested $1,000 in the idea and paid someone to launch the podcast. When I finally put some money on the line, a tangible commitment to making that dream come true, I broke through The Edge. As soon as I took that first step, I was all in! I knew if I put my money on the line, I would follow through. (Funny how money can do that.) Things started coming together and happening for my good. Guests and opportunities popped up all over—because I was looking for them. Because I was doing the thing. Because I conquered my edge. As I write this book, I am nearing three hundred episodes of the *Never Stop Getting Better* podcast.

THE LESSON: GET TO THE OTHER SIDE!

Right before a breakthrough, it almost always gets really hard. That's where most people stop, turn around, and go home. What are *you* going to do when you hit a wall? When you approach The Edge?

Here are five things to do at The Edge:

1. You are going to keep moving forward. Endure, persist, and get back up.
2. You will embrace the suck. It's part of the process—the sucky struggle—but on the other side of the suck is something good. Accept it, keep going, and you'll get there!
3. You are gonna use your mistakes as feedback. There is no failure, only learning opportunities. Ask yourself, "What can I learn from this? How do I adjust?"
4. You will remind yourself that fear is just a feeling, and it's one you can deflect or defeat. This is supposed to be scary. Anything worth doing is. Feel it, acknowledge it, keep moving.

5. You will stay coachable and make zero excuses. Listen, take guidance, adjust your approach, and stay accountable.

Everyone who's ever done anything worthwhile has faced The Edge. Parents starting over after loss, athletes chasing a dream, leaders stepping into new roles, business owners taking a risk, and students going back to school. They've all stared down the hard parts, the "suck," and kept going. They decided that their "willings" were equal to their "wants." If you *want* to win a state championship, lose ten pounds, whatever it may be, you have to be *willing* to do the uncomfortable work! On the other side of that discomfort, good things happen. That's how you break through any wall: You just don't quit until you get what you want!

We all go through times that are hard, and it would be a heck of a lot easier to just go sit our butts down in our cushy, plush recliner and kick up our feet. Instead, ask yourself, "What choices can I make right now to make things better? To make myself better? To reach my goal?" Then go do it. That's how you conquer The Edge.

THE CHALLENGE: DO "THAT ONE THING"

What's that one thing you've been dreaming about doing? That one thing that, deep down, you really want to do . . . but you're scared to do it? Maybe you feel insufficient. I don't know what's holding you back, but for whatever reason, you just haven't taken the leap even though you want to and know you should.

Your challenge today: Just do it. Do that "one thing."

Start a business.

Write a book.

Go back to school.

Make the phone call.

Start the conversation.

Launch the podcast.

You know exactly what it is. Your challenge today: DO. THAT. ONE. THING.

Need a little extra kick in the pants in order to finally make it happen? Name it. Email it to me at johnperry@neverstopgettingbetter.net, and I'll help hold you accountable. Or better yet, send me an email when it's done so I can celebrate with you!

Come on. Do the thing. Let's go!

CHAPTER 14

HATERS HATE

AT THE CONCLUSION of the 2015 season, having finished the year 4–7, someone called me while I was on my way to school and said, "They're talking about you on the radio this morning!"

I flipped over to the station just in time to hear a voice of a guy who had called in to the show to share his opinion (and called himself a friend of mine) saying, "It is time for Pearl to move on. John Perry is done. He cannot *get it done.*"

Well, that was a great way to start my day!

It was my eighth year at Pearl, and the previous seven years had seen us go 62–27, almost nine wins a year. So why were we having such a rotten season to begin with? Rewind a bit further, back to the conclusion of the 2014 season this time. We'd finished top ten in the state of Mississippi that year, and then we lost our twenty-five seniors, eighteen of whom were starters.

We also found out we were going into the largest classification of football, Class 6, and we knew we had less-than-super upcoming junior and senior classes. That meant that in 2015, we would go on to start eighteen sophomores! Knowing this was on the horizon, I set up a meeting with the Pearl superintendent, Dr. Morgigno. We discussed all these things, and I told him that 2015 would be a very tough year. But if he was okay with that, I was okay with that—because 2016/2017 could be very good. All was good.

Fast-forward to December 1, 2017. The horn buzzed, signaling the end of the game, and we had won the Class 6 State Championship over Starkville High School 21–17. Some people jumped the wall and ran onto the field. The first guy to grab me and give me a hug was, you guessed it, that same radio call-in fellow. No joke, the guy who said I was done was hugging me now, and he was so excited.

I had the thought of punching him but decided that probably wasn't the best action to take. So, I just . . . "let him."

Even back before Mel Robbins published her famous book *The Let Them Theory*, I had already learned that skill. I just let him, and I reminded myself that haters hate. It takes nothing for someone to talk smack. So what if he was an idiot, so what if he called in to the radio to say that stuff, so what if he was happy now. So what! It was a fantastic lesson for me to learn: People are just funny when it comes to sports. They are invested as if they are on the team. It's okay. Let them. As Abraham Lincoln once said, "This, too, shall pass."

That day, I learned to not worry myself over what others say. Others' reactions and words are just reflections of their own experiences. They may dog you today and hug you tomorrow. Let them!

One more lesson to be learned from the haters.

I have a friend (yes, we really are good friends today!) who emailed me six years ago after a junior varsity (JV) game at Branson High School. Long story short, he was upset that we got beat by Branson. He let me have it. I bet the email was 1,500 words. It was rather lengthy, and he left no stone unturned. The root of the email's message was that I was the worst JV coach in America. It was brutal.

What was my first instinct? To hit reply and send him a picture of that 2017 Class 6 State Championship ring. My first thought was very defensive, but having grown as a human and learned to Never Stop Getting Better, I asked myself an honest question: "Is there any truth to this, and can I use anything in this email to get better?"

To be honest, there *was* a lot of truth to the email. We worked on special teams for the first time on the bus ride down to the game. We spent very little time with our JV guys preparing for a game. (In my defense, in Mississippi, JV football was not very big, and we tried to cancel as many as possible. In Missouri, though, you play a full nine-game schedule, and it's considered real football.)

Well, after being honest with myself, I hit reply and said, "Thank you for the email. I will truly look at myself and see how I can get better. Again, thank you so much for the email." And I meant it! My next move was to pick up the phone and call the Yoda of high school football, Chris Yeager at Mountain Brook High School in Birmingham, Alabama. He was gracious enough to spend two hours with me on a Saturday via Zoom to make me a better JV coach.

Since that meeting, I believe we have only lost two JV games in five years. WE GOT BETTER!

And would it have happened had the email not been sent? Probably not. Would it have happened had I responded defensively? Probably not. Lesson for all of us: When we get a dirty email, are the target of an insulting call-in to a radio show, or are on the receiving end of anything that upsets us, take a quick inventory and see if there is any truth to it. Can you use any of that feedback, however harsh it may be, to get better? Remember, the purpose is always to Never Stop Getting Better. Thank you for teaching me that, Josh (wink wink).

THE LESSON: RESISTANCE IS A GOOD SIGN!

There's a strange blessing that comes with leadership played out under bright lights, with a scoreboard overhead, and a whole town watching. Being a head high school football coach is one of the few jobs where your work isn't tucked away in an office or hidden behind a PowerPoint slide. It's on full display in front of thousands. Every Friday night there is a public evaluation. Every call, every decision, every mistake, every success is right out there for the world to see.

And everyone in the stands thinks they could do it better.

In today's world, the arena is even bigger. The crowd isn't limited to the bleachers anymore. Social media has turned into a modern-day coliseum where anyone can grab a rock and throw it—no name, no face, no accountability required. Just a quick post, and a slice of someone's spirit can be chipped away by a person who never shook their hand, never watched a practice, never coached a kid, and never sacrificed a single hour for the program they critique.

For coaches, that can feel like an endless stream of noise: criticism, armchair expertise, and negativity. And when you pour your life into young men, pour your heart into a community, pour your energy into building something special . . . that can hurt. But if nobody cares enough to criticize you, you're probably not doing anything that matters!

One of the greatest mindset shifts any leader can make is this: Haters are proof of impact. You don't get haters by being average. You get haters when you're moving, building, growing, changing, elevating, influencing—when your life, your mission, your purpose is making enough noise to wake the opposition. Spiritually, that same principle applies.

If you believe in good and evil like I do, then you understand that Satan does not waste energy fighting those who pose no threat. "Be alert and of sober mind. Your enemy the devil prowls around like a roaring lion looking for someone to devour" (1 Peter 5:8). Satan goes after the difference-makers, the people trying to bring light into a dark world. The ones raising standards, building others up, strengthening families, and shaping communities.

If you're trying to live out God's plan, you will face resistance, often daily. Often from unexpected directions. And sometimes that resistance comes in the form of criticism, gossip, jealousy, and hate. When you understand this, you no longer see haters as obstacles. You start seeing them as confirmation that your life is headed in the right direction, and your work matters.

Coaching is not for the thin-skinned! The whistle comes with responsibility, expectations, leadership, vision, and the pressure of guiding young men through some of the most formative years of their lives. And it comes with criticism, both fair and unfair.

You don't get to choose whether the haters show up. You only get to choose whether they slow you down.

Every leader in history has faced resistance. Moses did. David did. Jesus himself did. Greatness in any form aggravates mediocrity, so when someone fires off a nasty comment online, when a rumor starts making the rounds, when someone with zero understanding of your work has a loud opinion . . . instead of being wounded, be reminded: "This is part of the calling."

It might sound crazy, but be grateful for the resistance, grateful for the struggle, grateful for the haters. They sharpen you, force you to clarify your purpose, and push you closer to God. They remind you that you're on the right path. Haters help you build mental toughness, emotional resilience, spiritual clarity, and leadership capacity. A coach without haters is a coach without impact, and a life without resistance is a life without growth.

When the critics speak up . . . when the online noise starts swirling . . . when the anonymous accounts show up with opinions . . . when the pressure mounts . . . just take a breath. Stand tall. Maybe even smile. Haters hate. Let them, and learn from it! You were not called to stay small just to make others comfortable. You were called to Never Stop Getting Better! Keep building, serving, leading, loving your team, and pursuing the mission God put on your heart.

THE CHALLENGE: LET THEM

The next time someone says something that offends you, just say this to yourself: "LET THEM."

The next time an insulting comment frustrates you, say: "LET THEM."

"Let them" is a response that allows you to be totally in control of your thoughts and actions. After you say that, follow it up with, "They are entitled to their opinion, and their opinion is no business of mine."

But also, before you move on, ask yourself two questions:

1. Is there any truth in this?
2. Is there anything I can learn from this to make me and/or my team better?

Criticism is more of a reflection of the person it is coming from, but letting the opportunity to at least try to learn from it pass would be a shame.

So now, I want you to think about the last time you were criticized. Write down the answers to both questions. *Is* there any truth to it? *Can* you learn anything from it that will make you or your team/family better?

Be honest. There's no harm in reflecting, learning, and letting go. The real shame lies in being defensive and missing the opportunity to learn, grow, and get better.

And remember: Just because someone says something does not mean they're an authority on the subject. LET THEM have their opinion. Do not allow yourself to dwell on the negative.

I still say, if you are not having people talk about you, you may not be doing enough! Anytime you do anything of substance in this world, you will find haters. It's just part of life, and in the digital world we now live in, it has only gotten easier for people to hate on others! Haters hate. LET THEM!

PART 4

BUILD THE TEAM

CHAPTER 15

FIND YOUR BOBBY HALL

NOW, I ALREADY told you the story of how I met and worked alongside the great Bobby Hall. Let me tell you a bit more about how that experience impacted me in the long run.

Back in 1999, Marcus Boyles (hall of fame coach) was hired at Pearl High School, where I coached as the offensive line coach. Marcus was a great coach, and I got to work with him for two years. But Pearl was not the right fit for Marcus and his family, so he left to work with Bobby Hall in Wayne County, Mississippi. Bobby had been Marcus's high school coach. He was legendary, and pretty soon I got an opportunity to work with him too. After I interviewed with Bobby a few times, we both knew it was a good fit, and I joined the coaching staff. I know Marcus vouched for me, so he played a critical role in getting me that job, and I will be forever thankful to him for that.

Whether that was by chance or the good Lord's intervention, the impact was that I learned how incredibly valuable it is to seek out people like Bobby: the greats, people further down the road who are ready and willing to share their expertise. *Mentors.* Learning football from Bobby Hall and Marcus Boyles taught me that *who* we learn from really, really matters.

In fact, my experience with Bobby was such a game changer that I decided I'd start finding more "Bobby Halls" as time went by. I got proactive, and I reached out to Rick Jones in Arkansas; Chris Yaeger and Mark Freeman in Alabama; Loren Montgomery in Bixby, Oklahoma; and many more of the best coaches in their respective regions. All I asked for was the opportunity to learn from them. I'd visit, I'd have long conversations, I'd observe. I asked questions, stayed curious, and learned all I could about how they did things and what helped them succeed.

Being around some of the best coaches out there made me a better coach over time. One hundred percent, no doubt about it. Who we spend time with matters more than we could possibly know. Deliberately seeking out mentors and positive examples to associate with can make all the difference.

For the life of me, I do not and will not ever understand why more people, in any profession, do not reach out to those further down the road than them and request their mentorship. Bobby Hall and Marcus Boyles were put into my life by chance and the good Lord, but *anyone* can reach out to people who are super successful in their field and ask them for advice.

One of the truths I have found is that the best of the best do not mind helping you. The best of the best got to the top the same way: Others helped them. If you ask someone for help and they decline, guess what? They are not that good anyway! *So what—now what?* Move on to the next. The best of the best love to give back by serving others. Do not let your ego or lack of self-confidence hold you back from growing, learning, and getting better! Make the call and connection, and you will be proud you did. Life is meant to be spent sharing with others, and what better way than sharing with the best of the best?

THE LESSON: BIRDS OF A FEATHER

One of the fastest ways to grow is to put yourself around people who are further down the road than you. You're not gonna rise any higher than the people you're learning from, so set your level high by associating with the best!

I learned not to be afraid to seek out mentors or admit I had something to learn from better, smarter, more experienced people to begin with! I'd call "the greats" up. I'd find out who the best coach in XYZ state was, then ask if I could just spend two or three days with them to learn absolutely everything I could. I didn't wait for opportunities to come to me; I went after the people who could help me grow.

I taught my children from a very young age, "Birds of a feather flock together." That's the power of association. Who you hang out with, who you learn from, and who you let influence you will shape your trajectory. Want to be great? Find people further down the path, study them, learn from their habits, and let their example raise your standard.

Yeah, there are thousands of reasons to hold back—pride, fear, intimidation—but growth doesn't come from staying comfortable. Growth comes from being bold enough to learn from the best, no matter what that takes.

Association accelerates transformation.

Who you hang out with . . .

Who you study . . .

Who you let influence you . . .

Who you allow to speak into your life . . .

All these choices shape your identity, your habits, your expectations, and your results.

If you want to be average, hang with average. If you want to be good, hang with good. If you want to be great, hang with great. Go find greatness and learn.

It's impossible to stay the same when the people around you are raising the standard daily.

THE CHALLENGE: ADD ONE!

Set up a meeting with someone further down the road than you. Just do it—and do it today! It can be a virtual connection or a real sit-down meeting in a coffee shop, whatever. Just find one person who you think highly of who could add value to your personal or professional life. Don't let fear slow you down, and do not let your ego tell you it's not needed. Just do it. Add one!

CHAPTER 16

VICARIOUS JOY

THERE'S A YOUTUBE clip that I love called "Anatomy of a Teammate."[23] The video shows the kind of unadulterated joy we humans *can* experience (if we choose to shift our mindsets) when we see someone else succeeding, just killing it: in life, on the field, whatever. Patrick Murphy, the head softball coach at the University of Alabama, shared this clip with me on the *Never Stop Getting Better* podcast, episode 58.

It's from an Alabama softball game, a playoff game where the pressure was high, and everything was on the line. Brittany Rogers, one of Alabama's star players, a four-time All-American, was in the lineup. She was fast and reliable. A leader. But late in the game, the coach pulled her out and sent in a sub to replace her. Alabama was down 2-0 versus Arizona State in the fourth inning of an elimination game.

If you've ever competed at any level, you know moments like that can hurt. Getting pulled out of the game doesn't feel good, and most athletes recognize the sting of wanting to be the one who comes through. Brittany could've sulked, kicked at the dirt, or buried her face in her hands. I would assume most of us would have pouted like a baby. ESPN did a split-camera view, hoping to catch Brittany throwing a fit or something newsworthy, I am sure. But that's not what happened. The video is famous for something else.

A few pitches later, Alabama's sub pinch hitter drilled a home run and won the game. The stadium erupted, of course, and with the split-screen camera angles, we could see Brittany's reaction. There's not a trace of bitterness there. She's ecstatic, absolutely losing her mind with happiness for her teammate and for her team! Jumping, screaming, pumping her fists, practically in tears, with not even a hint of that *should've been me* energy. Just pure, overflowing, unselfish, vicarious joy.

I love a good home run, but those happen all the time! This moment is an especially beautiful one because it captures what it means to be a teammate, and to be an elite teammate at that. Brittany had just been benched moments before, but there she is, celebrating her teammate's success like it's her own.

The teams that win are the teams that know how to celebrate each other. They feel vicarious joy when any member of the team succeeds, and that joy is at the heart of what makes a champion—and a truly incredible team! It's the glue that drives them onward and upward, growing stronger and better *together*!

THE LESSON: WINNING TEAMS CELEBRATE EACH OTHER

In Buddhism, there's a word for that kind of vicarious, sympathetic joy: *mudita*. It means feeling extreme joy in someone else's happiness, absolutely delighting in someone else's success—basically, it's the *opposite* of envy or jealousy! That's exactly what Brittany Rogers showed in that moment in the dugout.

Let's be honest, though. Most of us don't naturally think like that. It's human nature to be selfish, to compare and compete, but we need to learn to put that aside if we want to build teams that win! *Mudita* is at the core of a healthy, happy life; it's a crucial piece of what I like to call the champion mindset. You can't build an elite team culture without it!

When teammates genuinely celebrate one another, trust grows, comparisons shrink, competition becomes healthy instead of destructive, and the whole group's ceiling rises as they fight together instead of alone!

One of the topics I speak on fairly often is that champion mindset I mentioned above: What does it take to think like a champion? I think it's these three things:

- Mental toughness
- Chasing excellence
- *Mudita* (vicarious joy)

Mudita is right up there, alongside resilience and keeping an eye on the prize! You're not going to be a champion without it. Champions don't fear other people's success. They know that success is not some scarce resource, a pie we're all fighting to take a big ol' slice of before it runs out. (That's the power of an abundance mindset over a scarcity mindset, right?) You know that if your teammate shines, it doesn't dim the rest of the team. It lifts everybody up together. And that's part of why the best athletes, leaders, and humans surround themselves with people who make them better and lean into the inspiration of that excellence instead of making negative comparisons.

Brittany Rogers cheering her teammate's game-winning home run is champion thinking. She wasn't worried about how that awesome moment made her look. She wasn't embarrassed, because she knew that her teammate's win was *her* win too.

The teams that go deep into playoffs, the people that Never Stop Getting Better, the organizations that consistently perform, and the families that stay connected all share that same instinct. They celebrate each other out loud, often, and on purpose.

Again, I know it can be hard to shuck off our competitive, selfish natures and truly be a selfless teammate. There are a thousand reasons we hold back from celebrating others: fear, pride, insecurity, jealousy, that scarcity mindset. And you can't just tell yourself (or other people), "Be happy for each other!" and expect it to happen.

But there is a rhythm that can help get you there.

THE CHALLENGE: PRAISE IT, OWN IT

This practice came from Alabama's Coach Patrick Murphy, the same coach who coached Brittany Rogers. He calls it *Praise It, Own It*. It trains you in humility and generosity at the same time, and it'll give your team, group, or family an uncommon level of camaraderie.

Your challenge for this chapter is to start your own Praise It, Own It. You can do it with your family, the team you coach, your employees—any group you are a part of! At the end of each day, or practice, or family dinner, you gather together and go around the circle. Each member has the opportunity to do two things:

1. **Praise It:** You praise someone else in the group for something they did well that day. It could be effort, leadership, attitude, improvement; anything specific and genuine.
2. **Own It:** You own something you didn't do as well as you could have.

Here's an important tip: The leader always goes first. That sets the tempo. The leader models vulnerability and humility; you all spend a season praising each other and being held accountable, and that vicarious joy spreads like wildfire. That's the path to becoming a champion!

CHAPTER 17

CREATE THE CULTURE YOU WANT

ABOUT TEN YEARS ago now, I read *Start with Why* for the first time. It's an excellent book by Simon Sinek, and it's got a very real transformative message at its heart, an idea that wound up transforming how I coach, teach, and lead. The message is this: People don't buy *what* you do—they buy *why* you do it. Great leaders and great organizations inspire by starting with purpose, not products or plays. When your *why* is clear, your *how* becomes focused, and your *what* becomes powerful. Purpose drives loyalty, alignment, passion, and performance. If you want to move people—truly move them—start with the reason, not the result.

The book teaches readers and leaders all about defining what really matters: why we exist and what we were put on this earth to do! It's about vision, core values, and purpose. Those are the things meant to steer and direct our leadership, and we're meant to work them into the very fabric of our team's culture if we want to make any kind of difference. And thus, my journey toward my why began!

The journey to learn more about having a vision, values, and a purpose for our program became clearer when I called up the incredible Randy

Jackson and asked if I could visit and learn from him. I read his book, *Culture Defeats Strategy*, and was very intrigued by some of the things he was doing within his program. He was professing to be this "core values" guy at the time, known for teaching life skills and football skills side by side, and I wanted to see if all the things he wrote about were actually happening. I called him up, set up a visit, and the rest is history.

Much to my surprise, he *was* doing everything he wrote about in the book, and I got to watch him do it for a couple of days. It was amazing. So amazing that I wound up bringing him back to Pearl and had him go through his program with my coaches! And it was truly life-changing stuff. It set us up to be a program on another path, a path to changing lives and winning more games. Before Randy, I was driven by the thought of winning football games. After Randy, I was driven to win *kids*! And lo and behold, the winning took off!

Teaching life lessons around core values, vision, and behaviors—that kind of work really changes the game because it changes *how* you play the game. You want to lead? That's where you have to start. By changing the culture of those you're leading (and, of course, by modeling that culture by first doing the learning yourself!).

Here's a specific example of what I'm talking about: body language. When I brought Randy to Pearl and after we got his whole system integrated into our culture, we did things like this: If we had team members with terrible body language or a coach mentioned body language was a problem, we taught a lesson about it. There was a PowerPoint presentation and everything. We figured out that maybe no one had ever taught our players about body language or the impact it has. We wouldn't expect our kids to know how to run the veer without teaching them, so why would behavioral skills be any different? We couldn't expect our kids to know something we had never taught them! So we taught them, and it made a difference. Especially because we did it together. No longer were we just identifying problems, we were addressing them! Wow, what a thought, huh?

That's when football changed for me: when we shifted our focus and really nailed down our vision, our mission, and our core values. Our teams got better, and guess what? The kids' grades and behavior in school did too! That's the power of a rich, values-based culture. That's what leadership looks like. Change the human and you change the game!

When I arrived at Nixa, one of the first things I asked the other coaches was what problems their teams were facing. A lot of the answers went something like, "Our kids just aren't tough enough. They're downright soft." So, guess what we did some explicit lessons on? Toughness. What it means to be tough and how to avoid complaining and blaming others—parents, coaches, the other guys, whoever. There was a problem in the culture, so we targeted it. We transformed it. Because if you're a leader or a coach, and you can't solve the problems facing your team, they ought to get rid of you. Leaders take the first step. They change the culture. They pave the way for everyone on the team to Never Stop Getting Better.

That was the beginning of a journey to intentionally create a culture that drives the behaviors our team needs in order to succeed. And life has been trending up ever since!

THE LESSON: LEADERS → CULTURE → BEHAVIOR → RESULTS

Leaders create the culture that drives the behaviors that get the results. That's a fact. If you're a leader, you can let your bad habits, tendencies, and personality quirks create a culture without really paying much attention to what effect you're having on those around you. Or you can get intentional about it.

The cool thing about that progression—leadership forming culture, which forms behavior, which creates results—is that you can reverse engineer it! Whether you're leading a high school football team, a family, or a company, you can make it happen. Ask yourself these questions:

1. What result(s) do you want for your team?
2. What behavior(s) are going to produce that behavior?

3. What kind of culture fosters those behaviors?
4. Who's the leader that needs changing? Probably you, right? Start there.

Sure, you need to have some talent on your side, but I firmly believe that this process is effective whether we're talking about a bank, a tire shop, a church leadership team, or anything else.

Let's break down what it looks like to build a culture real quick. In my mind, it has everything to do with both (a) vision and (b) core values.

Building a positive culture begins with creating a vision that is so big and so good that other people are drawn to be a part of it. You want to set your team wondering, "Can I do that? Can I be a part of something this big and this cool?" From there, it's a quick hop, skip, and jump into instilling the beliefs, core values, and behaviors they need to succeed.

Core values are like those guardrails that help kids when they go bowling, the continuous bumpers set up to keep you out of the gutter. When you're about to make a life decision—whether you're in a tempting situation at a party, dealing with some tricky stuff with your kid, or making professional decisions—you run everything through that filter and look at everything through the lens of your core values. They steer you right. They keep you out of the gutter. So, we as a team have core values that guide all our actions.

It's the same in your personal life. What are your personal core values? When life gets challenging, what guides you to make the best decisions?

Here's an example of how your core values can play out in everyday life: Maybe you're at a red light, and the car next to you stalls. It's raining. You're late to work. You may just want to breeze on by, but you pause and think about your core values—curiosity, serving others, making a difference. Your decision just became very simple. You get out and help push that car to the gas station. It is truly fantastic what core values can do. They guide you to be your best self.

On the football team I coach today, we focus on one of our team's core values every day. We reflect on them and keep them in front of us all during the day. Maybe it's family, hard work, toughness. Whatever it is, we go through an explicit lesson on what the core value looks like, and we keep those guardrails firmly in place, keeping us all on the right path together! Because as leaders, that's how we achieve the results we want. We build a culture that creates the behaviors that make it happen. Culture defeats strategy. (Thanks, Randy Jackson.)

THE CHALLENGE: IDENTIFY YOUR CORE VALUES

Let's get your core values nailed down today. Here's what I want you to do:

1. **Scan the list below.** Go through slowly. Circle or highlight *any* value that speaks to you. Ask yourself, "Does this word define me right now?" You will feel it . . . trust your gut.

2. **Narrow it down.** Cut your marked list down by half, continuing to trust your gut as you determine which words don't resonate as strongly as the others. Then repeat, cutting it in half again and again until you only have two or three left.

3. **Pick your core two or three!** The few you have left are your non-negotiables. If everything else were stripped away, these are the values you still want your life defined by.

4. **Define them in your own words.** Take some time to write about what each means to you.

5. **Put them into action.** Write down how you plan to live these core values out on a daily level. How will people know these are your core values by what they see you doing and saying and expressing with your life?

Core Values List

Achievement	*Creativity*	*Fidelity*
Adventure	*Curiosity*	*Flexibility*
Altruism	*Daring*	*Flow*
Ambition	*Decisiveness*	*Forgiveness*
Appreciation	*Delight*	*Fortitude*
Authenticity	*Democracy*	*Freedom*
Awareness	*Dependability*	*Friendship*
Balance	*Determination*	*Frugality*
Beauty	*Devotion*	*Fun*
Belonging	*Dignity*	*Generosity*
Boldness	*Discipline*	*Gentleness*
Caring	*Discovery*	*Giving*
Certainty	*Diversity*	*Grace*
Challenge	*Drive*	*Gratitude*
Change	*Duty*	*Growth*
Charity	*Education*	*Guidance*
Clarity	*Effectiveness*	*Hard Work*
Collaboration	*Efficiency*	*Harmony*
Comfort	*Empathy*	*Health*
Commitment	*Empowerment*	*Helpfulness*
Community	*Energy*	*Holiness*
Compassion	*Enjoyment*	*Honesty*
Competence	*Enthusiasm*	*Honor*
Competition	*Equality*	*Hope*
Confidence	*Excellence*	*Hospitality*
Connection	*Excitement*	*Humility*
Consistency	*Experience*	*Humor*
Contribution	*Expertise*	*Impact*
Conviction	*Exploration*	*Independence*
Cooperation	*Fairness*	*Influence*
Courage	*Faith*	*Ingenuity*
Courtesy	*Family*	*Innovation*

Inquisitiveness
Insight
Inspiration
Integrity
Intelligence
Intensity
Intimacy
Joy
Justice
Kindness
Knowledge
Leadership
Learning
Legacy
Liberation
Listening
Love
Loyalty
Making a Difference
Mastery
Meaning
Moderation
Money
Motivation
Nurturing
Openness
Optimism
Order
Passion
Patience
Peace
Perseverance
Persistence
Personal Growth

Playfulness
Poise
Positive Attitude
Power
Practicality
Preparedness
Presence
Privacy
Professionalism
Prosperity
Punctuality
Purpose
Quality
Recognition
Relationships
Reliability
Resilience
Resourcefulness
Respect
Responsibility
Rest
Results
Risk-Taking
Sacrifice
Safety
Security
Self-Control
Self-Discipline
Self-Respect
Servant Leadership
Service
Sharing
Simplicity
Sincerity

Skillfulness
Solitude
Spirituality
Stability
Stewardship
Strength
Success
Support
Teamwork
Temperance
Thankfulness
Thoroughness
Thoughtfulness
Tolerance
Tradition
Tranquility
Transparency
Trust
Truth
Understanding
Uniqueness
Unity
Vision
Vitality
Wealth
Well-Being
Wisdom
Wonder
Zeal

CHAPTER 18

SERVE OTHERS AND MAKE A DIFFERENCE

IN CHAPTER 17, we talked about the importance of core values. My own life testifies to the power that lies in defining those values and filtering every step of your journey through them! My personal core values are summed up easily: stay curious, serve others, and make a difference.

I believe God put us on this earth to serve others and make a difference. Moving to Nixa, Missouri, gave us a great opportunity to live out those three core values. I invited my friend Phil Wickwar to write up this chapter's story on that topic. I believe he can tell this part better than I can. We often don't know the influence or effect we have on others. We get so busy doing life that we seldom reflect on the good things we have done. And, I also believe, we Americans stink at telling others we appreciate them! Well, Phil Wickwar breaks that mold. He has shared what our relationship has meant to him. Here it is, in his words:

> **Five years ago, I was in my mid-fifties. Life had been fantastic as well as challenging, a very similar journey as many of my peers. I was at a job that I had done for**

many years, and I felt extremely comfortable both personally and professionally. To be honest, I was about to find out that my biggest challenge was being stuck in a loop. I was too comfortable! You could almost say I was just functioning on autopilot at the time, and even though I was receiving positive feedback, sporadic achievements, and recognition for my efforts, something needed to change.

In February 2020, that change came in the form of a new head coach at the school where I was working.

We soon found out that the new leader of our football program was to be John Perry, a coach from Mississippi. John had produced great results at Pearl High School. John was understandably excited at his first meeting. Everyone likes enthusiasm . . . or "juice," as I was soon to hear it labeled. However, I was a veteran. I had seen enthusiasm come and go in many projects, the lives of friends, even in my own personal experiences. John's enthusiasm was sincere and inviting, but I was looking for a little more substance to invest in.

I sincerely believe that John's gift or strength, above all others (and he has many), is the casting of a vision, then constantly and tirelessly providing individuals the opportunity to join and grow with the process. I believe it is human nature to long for significance and purpose. Partnering with others can be hurtful and frustrating. Those who stay positive, with a clear mission and servant leadership, are the ones who can experience success and achievement at a much larger scale than if working independently.

Two things I observed that immediately made me want to commit to John's vision and mission:

1. A focus on the process and not the product. The ultimate goal serves as direction, but the focus is daily routines that, metaphorically, allow us to take a 1 percent step toward the ultimate goal. That 1 percent model provides you the opportunity to win daily! Also, John showed me the need to evaluate and make changes to anything that needed changing: responsibilities, mindsets, or negative habits that prevent those daily accomplishments from happening. This allows for time to evaluate and adjust to create success tomorrow.

2. The creation of a growth mindset. Be curious and never stop learning! The science behind the mind adapting to calculated stressors as well as intentional positive thoughts was parallel to many of the disciplines I had learned about the human body, as I had spent more than thirty-five years pursuing strength and fitness both personally and professionally. Because of the connection of the processes, I easily accepted the science and began doing my best to systematically embrace behaviors in pursuit of a higher level of mental wellness.

For me, everything really began when I adopted John's recommended routines of reading daily and committing to a gratitude journal. As the pursuit continued, I added in some awareness of E + R = O (a true life-changer for me!). Never Stop Getting Better was chased daily! I began having a personal vision and working to find my core values ([1] curiosity, [2] humility, [3] serving others) and intentionally monitoring and changing my self-talk. John introduced me to these habits, and many more, and they have added great value to my life.

The routines you commit to help maximize your experience daily, make you enormously more significant to others that you interact with, and prepare you to flourish in both bountiful and challenging times in your life. As an added bonus, I have been applying my learnings to my spiritual life. I am currently experiencing the absolute best relationship with Jesus Christ that I have had since dedicating my life to him more than thirty-five years ago. Growth in any area of your life takes a vision and intentional positive routines for growth to occur! And, as another bonus, John has become a fantastic friend with a beautiful family that continues to provide support, and he is a fantastic example of winning by growing self and serving others.

THE LESSON: A HEART OF SERVICE

The lesson for this chapter is a simple one. True significance comes from serving others and from having a positive impact on those around you. The purpose of everything that has been discussed in this book is for you to Never Stop Getting Better so you can show up for the people in your life and add value to them. It is not about how great you can be alone; it's about how much value you can add to your family, friends and coworkers. We grow so we can grow others.

I believe that is what God put us on this earth to do—to be the best version of ourselves so we can serve others. Pretty simple takeaway: Get better so you can add value to those you love.

"For even the Son of Man did not come to be served, but to serve, and to give his life as a ransom for many" (Mark 10:45).

"Do nothing out of selfish ambition or vain conceit. Rather, in humility value others above yourselves, not looking to your own interest but each of you to the interest of the others . . ." (wise words from Philippians 2:3–4).

THE CHALLENGE: ASSESS YOUR IMPACT

Take the next week for this one. At the end of each day, sit down and reflect on these questions in writing:

1. Did I do good in the life of a fellow human today?
2. Did I do something to make life *worse* for someone else?
3. What can I do tomorrow to have a bigger, brighter, better impact on the people around me?

CHAPTER 19

THE GREAT EXPERIMENT

O N JANUARY 30, 2020, I was introduced as the new head football coach at Nixa High School in Nixa, Missouri.

On February 25, we held our first Leadership Academy before school.

On February 26, we held our first Quarterback Academy (also before school).

In March, COVID-19 shut the world down. But the experiment had already begun!

We had spent twelve years at Pearl High School, my alma mater, and we never thought we would leave. Coaching at your old school is a special thing, and I loved the job and community. But the opportunity to take on a new challenge was intriguing! The idea of taking everything we had learned at Pearl and applying it at a place where we knew no one was both exciting and intimidating. Scary, but interesting. After a lot of prayer and family conversations, we made the decision to move to Nixa, Missouri. And just like that, the experiment was on.

I was introduced to the players and parents in the Nixa High School library on February 24. The very first slide I put on the screen was our vision statement: "To become the best football program in the state of Missouri and build leaders." It was bold. I knew that. But I had stood in front of another group of young men years earlier at Pearl and shared the same kind of vision, and I had watched it come to life.

People don't have to believe in the vision right away. They do have to believe that *you* believe in it. And I did, wholeheartedly. If it worked once, why couldn't it work again? Why not Nixa? It could, and it did!

The vision was set and so was our direction. The vision gives us our North Star! Next was time for our core values, which shape behavior. We didn't just list values, but we also started to teach them. Each day of the week carried a vision, and with that an expectation as to how our team was going to behave.

- *Monday:* Hard work
- *Tuesday:* Family
- *Wednesday:* Commitment
- *Thursday:* Positive attitude
- *Friday:* Tough

These values became our daily filter for how we practiced, how we coached, how we led, and how we responded.

Next came our mission—our why—and it was simple: "We will play football in Nixa to make our families, our school, and our community proud."

The next thing we did was start installing the systems that would support the culture we needed to be successful. And we knew it came from more than just slogans on the walls. It comes from each of our systems executed consistently. We committed to getting 1 percent better every day, and we built processes and systems to support that belief:

- Morning weight room sessions
- Development of eighth-grade athletes by coming in before school in the offseason
- Leadership Academy
- Quarterback Academy
- Purposeful position meetings
- Weekly messages and storytelling
- Daily reinforcement of core values
- Mental performance training and eventually hiring a mental performance coach
- Education on sleep, nutrition, habits, and routines
- Book studies: *Chop Wood Carry Water* and *The Twin Thieves*
- Chasing Excellence daily
- Guest speakers: Damon West, Walter Bond, etc.
- Zoom sessions during COVID-19

Drip by intentional, disciplined drip, we added to our culture with the purpose of creating the behaviors we needed to be successful.

What began as a bold experiment became a proven process. Back-to-back state championship appearances in 2024 and 2025 were the products of a clear process! When the vision is bold, the values are lived, and the systems are consistent, growth is inevitable. The experiment was never just about football. It was about belief. It was about leadership. It was about doing the work every single day. And we were only getting started!

THE LESSON: EVERYTHING MATTERS

To change culture, *everything* matters. Whether it's a workplace, a home, a school, a church, or a football program, culture isn't shaped by one big speech, one rule, or one defining moment. It's built through the daily compounding of small behaviors that consistently reinforce the vision you've laid out. Culture starts with leadership! You must live the values first before you ever expect others to follow them. From there, culture grows through intentional repetition—finding ways to *drip* the right behaviors into the organization day after day.

Great culture does not happen by accident, and it does not happen fast. If you start doing the work today—intentionally, consistently, and patiently—you can begin to see meaningful results in one to two years. That's a good thing, though! Anything built overnight won't last.

Culture is created by stacking:

- Small actions
- Clear expectations
- Consistent standards
- Relentless follow-through

The key is identifying the *little things*, the daily or weekly habits that reinforce who you want to be. When repeated long enough, those behaviors begin to shape beliefs. Beliefs drive behavior. And behavior drives results. That was the Great Experiment at Nixa. We didn't chase quick fixes. We committed to the process. Over time, the culture began to carry the program forward. Everything mattered—because everything still does.

THE CHALLENGE: STACK THE DAYS

Choose three small behaviors that reflect your desired culture. Commit to doing them every day for twenty-one days.

Examples:

- Start every meeting on time
- Acknowledge one person daily
- End the day with one note of gratitude
- Send one positive message to the group

PART 5

CONCLUSION

CHAPTER 20

GROW YOUR GARDEN

MY GRANDDAUGHTER GEORGIA and I are basically farmers nowadays.

Okay, okay, not really. All the wonderful knowledge I could share with you about agricultural best practices could fit in a teaspoon, with room to spare. But I tell you what, the little tomato and pepper plants Georgia and I have taken to growing together have provided us with some great learning opportunities. They've given us the gift of quality time spent together, and they have taught us several things over the past few years. In fact, my time gardening alongside that little girl provides the perfect metaphor for what I mean when I say Never Stop Getting Better.

Gardening teaches you that you just have to *keep on grinding*. You have to do the same old thing over and over and over. Day after day, you water that dirt, until eventually you'll find yourself watering the tiny, insignificant-looking plant that pops up. As time wears on, it feels like not a dang thing is happening. You also have to pull the weeds so they don't take over the growth you are really looking for. Georgia loves to water and pull the weeds. She loves the process. (That's another lesson our garden has taught us: You must love the process.)

Then, all of a sudden, there's the fruit, and you're watching some cherry tomatoes ripen. You keep on working and waiting. As soon as they're ready, you get to eat them, sweet and fresh and right off the vine! (No one else in the family gets to enjoy our grape tomatoes, though; Georgia devours them all.)

Isn't that just like life? You plant seeds every day and you don't know when (or if!) things'll ever grow. But I can promise you, if you plant and water and fertilize that garden of yours, and if you tend to it religiously, eventually something good is going to come!

It makes me think of the Chinese bamboo plant. When you plant the seed, nothing seems to happen. For the first year, you water it, fertilize it, and care for it . . . nothing breaks the surface. In the second year, the same routine—still nothing. Third year—no visible growth. Fourth year—nothing you can see. Many people would quit well before this time. They would assume the seed is bad, quit watering, and walk away.

But in the fifth year, something incredible happens. The Chinese bamboo tree shoots up eighty to ninety feet in just a few weeks. So the question is: Did the bamboo grow ninety feet in five weeks or five years? The truth is, the bamboo was doing the invisible work during those first four years, developing an extensive root system underground. Without those roots, the bamboo would never be able to support its rapid growth or withstand strong winds.

Put the good stuff in and weed out the bad stuff. Consistently. Daily. There'll be results! Believe it, and don't quit! Never Stop Getting Better!

THE LESSON: TEND YOUR GARDEN

It was almost twenty years ago that I started my habit of reading every morning. After ten years of that one daily practice, I started getting the opportunity to speak to teams on mental fitness, good habits, stuff like that. Now, nearly twenty years in, I'm leading leadership sessions for Central Bank and being asked to speak to various groups multiple times per month. All because I made the choice to wake up a bit earlier and read a bit more.

Start planting those seeds. Fertilize them and water them over and over until harvest time comes. You know why people fail? They get impatient. They're looking too far into the future, and they don't see the results coming as quickly as they want, so they give up. Now me, maybe it's just that I'm not smart enough to really think too far into the future. I got an 18 on the ACT, but maybe that short-sighted focus and attention span of mine work in my favor here, because it's the bullish choice to just do the thing, day after day, that made the magic happen for me.

Life's a garden. You have to stay patient and realize you will not see results immediately. Just plant wisely, water daily, and trust the harvest.

THE CHALLENGE: GET GROWING!

All right, my friend. This is it, your very last challenge of the book!

For the next thirty days, choose one area of your life where you'd like to grow (faith, marriage, skills, fitness, leadership, relationships, etc.).

1. Define your seed. Write down the one thing you're planting. Be specific: "I will spend ten minutes reading Scripture daily," "I will connect with one player every day outside of practice," or whatever it is that you want to improve.
2. Water daily. Commit to completing that one small, consistent action every day!
3. Track it. Use a journal, planner, or habit tracker app to check it off the list each day.
4. No digging. Resist the urge to judge your progress on a daily basis. Don't "dig up the seed." Trust the process!

5. Reflect. After the thirty days are up, spend some deep, thoughtful time looking back and writing about what shifted, grew, and strengthened in you.

The prize doesn't go to the most talented guy. It goes to the one who just shows up and does the work! Water your garden every single day. Be patient, be consistent, and trust the process. Even if you don't see anything for weeks, eventually, *bam*: You'll get that tomato, and it'll be fabulous.

CHAPTER 21

IT'S HALFTIME

LET'S PRETEND THAT as you finish this book, we are at halftime of life. If you are around forty years old, you really are at halftime, or close to it! Halftime is that rare moment when the noise pauses, the chaos settles, and everyone has a chance to breathe. The scoreboard is what it is. The first half has already been played, and no amount of wishing will change it.

Here's a little secret: No one ever remembers who was winning a game at halftime. I guarantee you, you can't name a halftime score of one Super Bowl or National Championship Game. But halftime gives you something far more valuable than a reset—it gives you a chance to adjust. So let's have you use *your* halftime to adjust your life.

Because life has halftimes too! And whether you realize it or not, if you're reading this right now, you're standing in one. This is a pause point. A moment to reflect, to assess yourself honestly, and to decide how you want the rest of the game of life to look. Halftime isn't about panic or blame, and it's not about starting over. It's about making small, intentional adjustments that lead to a better second half and a win at the end of the game.

Great teams don't throw out the entire playbook at halftime. They don't chase miracles or overhaul everything they believe in. They identify what's working, fix what's broken, and recommit to playing the next quarter with more clarity and purpose. The same principle applies to life. Most people don't need a complete transformation. They need simplicity, consistency, and the courage to do a few things better than they've been doing them. Can we take a few simple things, install them for the second half, and Never Stop Getting Better?

The truth is, how you finish matters far more than how you start! The first half of your life, however you define it, has already happened. Some of it was filled with wins and momentum. Some of it came with disappointment, loss, or regret. That's part of the deal. You aren't defined by the opening kickoff. You're defined by how you respond when the game gets tight, when fatigue sets in, and when effort becomes a choice instead of a feeling.

Championship teams are built in the second half, and so are meaningful lives. The third quarter often tells the real story. It reveals who made the better adjustments and who drifted. It exposes habits, discipline, and belief. You don't have to win the entire game in the third quarter, but you do have to win the quarter. Momentum is built there, one possession at a time.

The adjustments that matter most are usually the simplest ones. Simplifying your life creates energy. Controlling what you can control restores confidence. Committing to getting just 1 percent better (14:24) each day compounds in ways you can't see immediately but will eventually feel deeply. Recommitting to your habits—how you sleep, move, think, and prepare—shapes your future far more than any goal ever will. And increased awareness of your inputs, your environment, and your self-talk becomes the gateway to lasting growth.

There is something powerful about people who finish well. Not perfectly or loudly, but intentionally. Finishing strong doesn't ignore the past; it learns from it. It doesn't rush the future; it prepares for it. It focuses on doing the next right thing, again and again, especially when no one is watching.

That's the purpose of this book. Not to overwhelm you or to demand that you change everything overnight, but to give you a few tools worth installing into your life right now. Take what fits, practice it daily, trust the process. Let the small adjustments do their work over time.

You're at halftime. The clock hasn't expired, the game isn't over, and there's still plenty of energy left in you. Make the adjustments and start the third quarter with intention. Commit to finishing stronger than you started. Because in the end, the stories that matter most aren't about how someone began—they're about how they finished. Never Stop Getting Better!

AFTERWORD

JOHN AMAZES ME daily with his constant pursuit of getting better. He encourages me to get better, be the person that God wants me to be, and to love unconditionally. John isn't perfect, but he is perfect for me, and we are perfect together. He is my person, my ride or die, my best friend, and I thank God every day that we have the kind of relationship we have. John makes me want to be better.

Things have not always been as good as they are now. John and I came into this marriage over thirty years ago young, dumb, and selfish kids. We both had ideas of what marriage should look like, and of course, we thought only our own ideas were correct! We tried to run our marriage the way our parents had run theirs and quickly found out that didn't work for us. We had to fight, cry, laugh, and all the things in between to figure it out! We are still a work in progress, but that makes us even better. We both work daily to try and do something that makes the other person's life just a little better.

The way I have seen John improve himself over the past fifteen years is truly remarkable. At his core, John is an introvert. He listens, he watches, and he observes the world around him. I am the opposite; I'm a talker and the most unobservant person around. John has worked very hard to be comfortable with being center stage and having so much attention on him. By watching him, I have learned that sometimes being quiet and observing is the best thing for everyone around. John is generous beyond compare; I am not! He would give anything to the people he loves, whereas I'm much stingier and more selfish. It's no wonder the kids always ask him for money and not me! John has taught me that material possessions are not mine to begin with, that God is letting me borrow them, and I sure am not taking them to heaven with me. I did say that I am still working on this, right?

John shows deep, unconditional love. This has been shown time and time again with our families. I am ashamed to say that there have been times when I had been hurt so deeply by the actions and words of others that I was ready to cut them out of our lives, or at least I thought I was. I can go on a silent, ignoring streak with the best of them, but not John. He continues to let the person who wronged him feel loved and appreciated. He works to get to the core of the problem and is ever forgiving, even if it means he is the one who has to apologize and change his behavior. He gently encourages me to do the right thing and forgive the way Jesus wants me to. He doesn't push or force me to forgive, but seeing the peace he has makes it much more inviting to do the same.

I have always had a great sense of pride when I watch John coach, speak, or engage with others. I am in awe because I would rather eat spinach than get in front of a group of adults and do something! The thing that almost makes my heart burst with pride, though, is the way our granddaughter, Georgia, looks at him. She loves me and wants to be around me, but there is no one quite like her Poppa! There is something so true and innocent about the way she loves him. He is pretty crazy about her too!

John has worked hard on making his dreams come true. He has transformed losing teams into winning teams; built men out of boys; and changed hard, stubborn attitudes into loving souls—but most of all, he has changed into the best version of himself. This is a relentless pursuit that he strives to reach every single day. This book is a work of love and servanthood. He wants to share what he has learned with as many people as possible. I pray that John's life and experiences can affect you the way he has affected me and our family.

—STEPHANIE PERRY

ACKNOWLEDGMENTS

FIRST AND FOREMOST, I would like to thank God for always being in my corner. Life has thrown its fair share of challenges our way, but God has been faithful through them all—even in the moments when we were not doing our part to honor him. His grace has been constant, his presence unwavering. God is good.

Thank you to my wife—my ride or die—Stephanie. From day one, she has given me the opportunity to chase success in life and coaching. We've ridden the roller coaster of life together, and somehow, we've grown closer through every twist and turn. I've often said, "You either have a great wife and a chance to be a successful coach, or you don't." I do. Thank you, Steph.

One of the greatest joys in life is watching your children grow and succeed in their own journeys. Haley and J—thank you for giving me the opportunity to be your dad and for allowing me the grace to grow as a dad along the way. We clearly missed the Parenting 101 manual. Parenting is hard, and we learned through plenty of trial and error.

Thank you for overcoming *us* and for blessing us with the people you have become. We love you both dearly and could not be prouder.

Now, let's get to the real joy—**GEORGIA** (lol). Becoming a grandparent has been one of the greatest blessings of our lives. It's been a chance to do everything right from the start. She is the most awesome kid alive and has brought more joy to our family than we ever imagined. As of this writing, we have another grandchild on the way—**CASH**—who may already be here by the time you're reading this. I have no doubt he will double our love and joy.

My parents, Steve and Judy Perry, are the reason I am doing what I am doing. I was blessed with parents who modeled strong values and loved my brothers and me endlessly. They took us to every practice, every game, and every sport—year after year. We played them all, whether we wanted to or not! I played ball until I was twenty-two years old, and I think they missed exactly one game—and that was only because my dad was preaching at his sister's funeral. Through thirty-two years of coaching, they have missed very few games. They have been role models that many kids never get, and I am forever grateful for the example they set. Love y'all.

Most people have stories about their in-laws—and I'm no exception (lol). Bobby Brothers, whose life and legacy still bless our family, and Ellen Brothers, who continues to show up or watch every game, have been an incredible blessing to me. I'm grateful for their influence, their love, and for allowing me to date their daughter for the past thirty-four years.

I am incredibly grateful for the many coaches who have shaped my life. I've been blessed with more than I deserve. Bruce Merchant, my high school coach, gave me my first job and made a lasting impact on my life—one I could never fully repay. Gene Murphy gave me the opportunity to play at Hinds Community College and, more importantly, put up with my behavior while I was there. Coach, I owe you an apology and a thank-you. Larry Richmond took a chance on me by allowing me to walk on at Harding University—and without that opportunity, I would never have met my better half.

As an offensive lineman, my O-line coaches played a huge role in my development: the late Gavin Lott, J. Mike Smith, and James Frank. Learning from so many great coaches has been a blessing, and having the opportunity to coach alongside Bruce Merchant, Bobby Hall, and Marcus Boyles gave me a head start in this profession. To every assistant coach I've worked with along the way—thank you. This profession takes a tribe, and I've been fortunate to be part of a great one.

I'd also be foolish not to mention a few of my youth coaches who got me started early and pointed me in the right direction: Bo Jeffcoat, John Bradshaw, and my dad. The Saints and the Bengals were tough to beat fifty years ago (lol). Thank you.

I like to say it takes three things to be successful in high school football: strong administration, great assistant coaches, and talent. I've been blessed to work for some of the very best administrators. The first superintendent to give me a job was the late Dr. David Sistrunk in Kosciusko, Mississippi—truly a godsend. My first principal, the late Mrs. Jerlyn Jackson, taught me what it meant to truly have someone's back—and she always had mine.

I'm thankful for every administrator I've had the privilege to work with and learn from: Matt Dillon, Ray Morgigno, Chris Chism, Gearl Loden, David Kelly, Richard Smithhart, Brandon Clark, the late William Dodson, and Greg Ladner. Each of you played an important role in my growth.

I've had many mentors and hesitate to name names because so many people have poured into me, but here's a short list: Chris Yeager, Rick Jones, Dr. Rob Gilbert, Randy Jackson, Will Hall, Randy West, and Terry Hughes. Thank you for your time, wisdom, and servant hearts. You have blessed me.

A special thank-you to the late, great *Mr. Pearl,* Ray Rogers. What a gift he was to me and so many others. One of the proudest moments of my career came each year when he would tell the Pearl Pirate story to the incoming freshmen and say, without fail, "I am so proud to have one of our own—and the first Pearl graduate ever—as our head football coach, John Perry." I could hear the pride in his voice every time. Ray announced Pearl High School football games for fifty-six years—yes, *fifty-six*. He was also the first quarterback on the very first Pearl team. He and Mrs. Shirley—who is as beautiful today as ever—truly were Mr. and Mrs. Pearl. Thank you for the honor.

I would also like to thank the many friends who have walked alongside us through the years. Life would not be the same without you. While there are too many to name, a few special ones include the McHenrys, Potts, Hayes, Wickwars, Worrells, Welches, and Samantha Steen. Your love and friendship have meant more to our family than you know.

Lastly, thank you to all the players and parents who have come through our programs. Without you, we would never get to do what we do. Football is a tough sport played by tough people, and I've been honored to coach many of them. Thank you.

ABOUT THE AUTHOR

JOHN PERRY is the head football coach at Nixa High School in Nixa, Missouri. In six seasons, he has led Nixa to a record of 64–11, with four COC championships, three district championships, and two Class 6 state runner-up finishes. He has been named Central Ozark Conference Coach of the Year four times and was selected to coach in the Under Armour All-America Game this past January. He coached the number one player in America, Jackson Cantwell, who was recently named the 2025–2026 Gatorade National Football Player of the Year.

John is a certified Mental Performance Mastery Coach, as well as the host of the *Never Stop Getting Better* podcast. He is also a John Maxwell certified speaker, trainer, and coach. With a wealth of experience, John has become a sought-after speaker, sharing his insights and expertise at a diverse range of events. He also teaches mental fitness and leadership skills to businesses throughout Springfield, Missouri, and was recently named the winner of the 2025 Kathy Whitworth Service to Education Award. He serves on the board of advisors for the Chuck Wiley Foundation and the Nixa Education Foundation.

John came to Nixa from Pearl High School in Pearl, Mississippi, where he served as head football coach and assistant athletic director for twelve years. In 2017, Perry led Pearl to the first state championship in school history. Perry has spent over thirty years molding and coaching championship teams. He has spent a combined twenty-three years as a head coach at Kosciusko, Pearl, and Nixa, amassing 211 career wins. Perry has received numerous coach of the year awards, led his teams to ten region championships, earned two south state runner-up finishes, and achieved two south state championships. Additionally, in 2017, he and his team became only the third school in Mississippi high school football history to finish 16–0. In 2018, Perry became the winningest coach in Pearl history with 101 victories.

Perry graduated from Pearl High School (1989), Hinds Community College (1991), and Harding University (1994). He has been married to the former Stephanie Brothers of Atlanta, Georgia, since 1995. They have a daughter Haley, a son J, and a granddaughter Georgia.

ENDNOTES

1   John Perry, host, *Never Stop Getting Better,* episode 100, "Champion Mindset: Coach Paul Simmons on Culture and Expectations," May 16, 2024, 1 hour, 12 min., https://podcasts.apple.com/us/podcast /episode-100-champion-mindset-coach-paul-simmons-on /id1689147696?i=1000655760483.

2   Christina Comaford, "Got Inner Peace? 5 Ways to Get It NOW," *Forbes,* April 4, 2012, https://www.forbes.com/sites/christinecomaford /2012/04/04/got-inner-peace-5-ways-to-get-it-now.

3   Nancy Colier, "Negative Thinking: A Dangerous Addiction," *Psychology Today,* April 19, 2019, https://www.psychologytoday.com /us/blog/inviting-monkey-tea/201904/negative-thinking- dangerous-addiction.

4   Pierre Khawand, "47% of the Time Our Minds Wander," YouTube Short, December 15, 2025, https://www.youtube.com/shorts /gVd8Hqhhc7s.

5 Craig Groeschel, "Best Way to Avoid an Overwhelming Life," sermons.love, July 11, 2022, https://sermons.love/craig-groeschel/11692-craig-groeschel-best-way-to-avoid-an-overwhelming-life.html.

6 Julia Naftulin, "Here's How Many Times We Touch Our Phones Every Day," *Business Insider*, July 13, 2016, https://www.business insider.com/dscout-research-people-touch-cell-phones-2617-times-a-day-2016-7.

7 Craig Groeschel and Wayne Chappell, *Heal Your Hurting Mind: Biblical Hope for Anxiety, Depression, Burnout, and the Emotions No One Talks About* (Zondervan, 2026).

8 Groeschel and Chappell, *Heal Your Hurting Mind*.

9 Groeschel and Chappell, *Heal Your Hurting Mind*.

10 John Perry, host, *Never Stop Getting Better*, episode 28, "USC Trojans Leadership Coach Tim Kight Delivers a Masterclass on the 'R' Factor," September 7, 2023, 1 hour, 11 min., https://podcasts.apple.com/us/podcast/episode-28-usc-trojans-leadership-coach-tim-kight-delivers/id1689147696?i=1000627043716.

11 *Sly*, directed by Thom Zimny (Netflix, 2023).

12 Matt Walker, *Why We Sleep: Unlocking the Power of Sleep and Dreams* (Scribner, 2017).

13 Sleep Doctor, "How to QUICKLY Fall Back Asleep in the Middle of the Night (As You Age)," YouTube video, 10:21, January 28, 2025, https://youtube/NN4wWO2kSY8.

14   Cheryl Robinson, "New Year's Resolutions Aren't Enough. Developing New Habits Is the Real Flex," *Forbes*, December 30, 2025, https://www.forbes.com/sites/cherylrobinson/2025/12/30/new-years-resolutions-arent-enough-developing-new-habits-is-the-real-flex.

15   "Truman Quotes," Truman State University, accessed February 5, 2026, at https://www.truman.edu/about/history/truman-quotes.

16   "70 Remarkable Jim Rohn Quotes for Achieving More in 2026," *Success Magazine*, September 17, 2017, https://www.success.com/17-remarkable-quotes-by-jim-rohn.

17   John M. Jennings, "Are You in the Top Half of Readers? The Surprising Reading Habits of American Adults," April 26, 2024, https://johnmjennings.com/are-you-in-the-top-half-of-readers-the-surprising-reading-habits-of-american-adults.

18   John Perry, host, *Never Stop Getting Better*, episode 170, "Breaking Barriers: Tyson Lee's Journey of Faith, Family, and Resilience," January 16, 2025, 1 hour, 7 min., https://podcasts.apple.com/us/podcast/episode-170-breaking-barriers-tyson-lees-journey-of/id1689147696?i=1000684199201.

19   John Perry, host, *Never Stop Getting Better*, episode 78, "Embracing Your Role: Maximizing Opportunities with Coach Eliah Drinkwitz," February 29, 2024, 41 min., https://podcasts.apple.com/us/podcast/episode-78-embracing-your-role-maximizing-opportunities/id1689147696?i=1000647496517.

20 John Perry, host, *Never Stop Getting Better*, episode 82, "Building Champions: Inside the Coaching Career of Dan Lanning at University of Oregon," March 14, 2024, 41 min., https://podcasts .apple.com/us/podcast/episode-82-building-champions -inside-the-coaching/id1689147696?i=1000649155447.

21 John Perry, host, *Never Stop Getting Better*, episode 150, "The Winning Mindset: Lessons from NBA Legends with Alan Stein Jr.," November 7, 2024, 55 min., https://podcasts.apple.com/us /podcast/episode-150-the-winning-mindset-lessons-from-nba /id1689147696?i=1000676023538.

22 Sean Glaze, "A Story About Cowards, Heroes, Boxing, and Heart," Great Results Team Building, accessed April 15, 2026, https:// greatresultsteambuilding.net/story-cowards-heroes-boxing-heart.

23 Randall Hunt, "Anatomy of a Teammate," YouTube video, 7:49, https:// www.youtube.com/watch?v=g_iM05vVP84&t=2s.